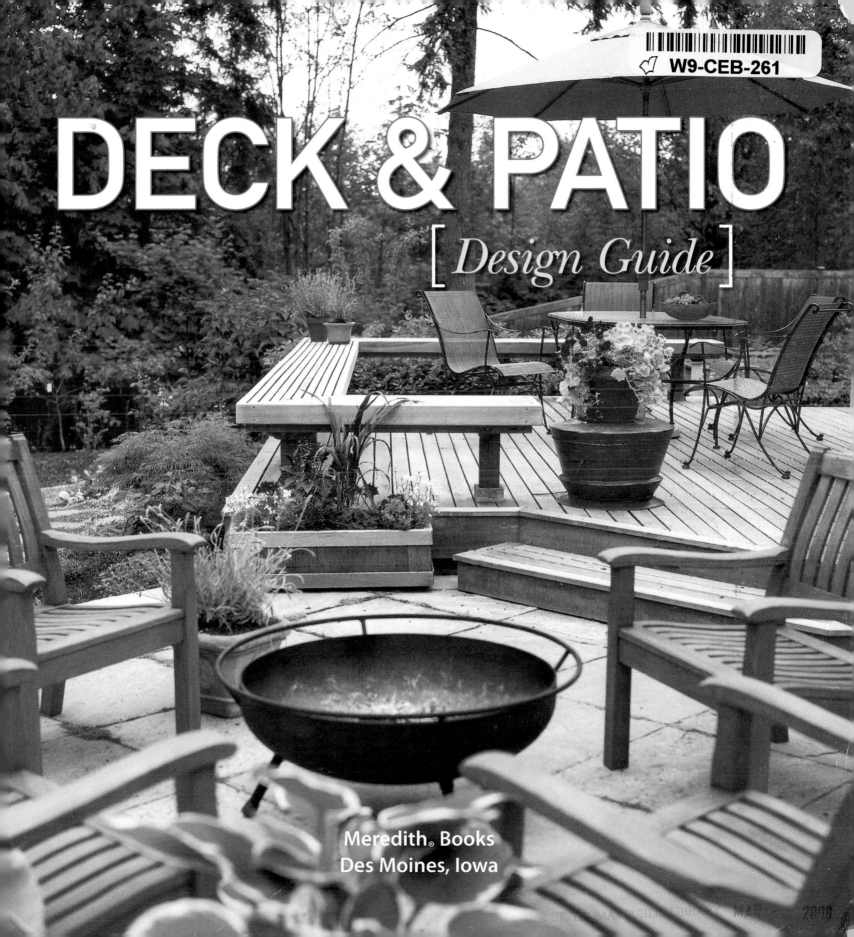

DECK & PATIO

[*Design Guide*]

Meredith₀ Books
Des Moines, Iowa

Better Homes and Gardens® Deck & Patio Design Guide

Editor: Paula Marshall
Associate Design Director: Todd Emerson Hanson
Contributing Project Manager, Editor, and Writer: Lexicon Consulting, Inc.
Contributing Graphic Designer: On-Purpos, Inc.
Copy Chief: Terri Fredrickson
Copy Editor: Kevin Cox
Publishing Operations Manager: Karen Schirm
Senior Editor, Asset & Information Management: Phillip Morgan
Edit and Design Production Coordinator: Mary Lee Gavin
Art and Editorial Sourcing Coordinator: Jackie Swartz
Editorial Assistant: Kaye Chabot
Book Production Managers: Pam Kvitne, Marjorie J. Schenkelberg,
   Mark Weaver
Imaging Center Operator: Ben Anderson
Contributing Copy Editor: Susie Fagan
Contributing Proofreaders: Sara Henderson, Nancy Ruhling, Lida Stinchfield
Contributing Indexer: Index Solutions, Stephanie Reymann

Meredith® Books
Editor in Chief: Gregory H. Kayko
Executive Director, Design: Matt Strelecki
Managing Editor: Amy Tincher-Durik
Executive Editor: Benjamin W. Allen
Senior Editor/Group Manager: Vicki Leigh Ingham
Senior Associate Design Director: Ken Carlson
Marketing Product Manager: Brent Wiersma

Executive Director, Marketing and New Business: Kevin Kacere
Director, Marketing and Publicity: Amy Nichols
Executive Director, Sales: Ken Zagor
Director, Operations: George A. Susral
Director, Production: Douglas M. Johnston
Business Director: Jim Leonard

Senior Vice Presdent: Karla Jeffries

Vice President and General Manager: Douglas J. Guendel

Better Homes and Gardens® Magazine
Editor in Chief: Gayle Goodson Butler
Deputy Editor, Home Design: Oma Blaise Ford

Meredith Publishing Group
President: Jack Griffin
Executive Vice President: Doug Olson

Meredith Corporation
Chairman of the Board: William T. Kerr
President and Chief Executive Officer: Stephen M. Lacy

In Memoriam: E.T. Meredith III (1933–2003)

Copyright © 2008 by Meredith Corporation, Des Moines, Iowa.
First Edition.
All rights reserved.
Printed in the United States of America.
Library of Congress Control Number: 2007933338
ISBN: 978-0-696-23607-5

Contents

DECK & PATIO
[*Design Guide*]

Offering valuable outdoor living space that family and friends will enjoy for years, decks and patios give new meaning to the sentiment "home is where the heart is." By taking the comforts of home outside, a well-placed deck or patio can serve as your home's crowning touch and increase your property value. Whether you choose a poolside patio oasis or a multilevel deck to accommodate large family get-togethers, *Deck & Patio Design Guide* will help you turn your dreams into reality by leading you through every step of the process.

It's time to unleash your imagination and begin dreaming about your ideal outdoor living space. The first step: Gather fresh ideas and inspiration from the decks and patios featured in Chapter 1, "Explore Your Options." From outdoor entertaining spaces to quiet retreats, you'll find a little bit of everything.

Once you're armed with ideas, let your needs and wants narrow your focus and jumpstart the planning process. Chapter 2, "Plan the Project," dives into the nitty-gritty of essential deck and patio prep: establishing a reasonable budget, hiring professionals, obtaining bids, and fully understanding the specifics of estimates and contracts. You'll also determine whether you can tackle the project yourself and learn to be assertive when working with pros.

Chapter 3, "Evaluate the Site," shows you how to design a deck or patio that makes the most of your property by taking advantage of property shape, slope, shade, and views. This chapter also explains how to incorporate existing landscaping and create visual harmony with your outdoor living spaces. Considering accessibility, traffic flow, and building code requirements early on can help you make important decisions later in the process.

If you go the deck route, Chapter 4, "Deck Basics," will guide you through the building process with helpful construction terminology, different decking and fastener options, and maintenance tips. Explore the abundance of possibilities for customizing your deck with railings, stairs and ramps, overheads, and built-ins.

Discover the most critical components needed to build a patio in Chapter 5, "Patio Basics." A detailed materials list will help you choose the right surface. And for a comfortable, pleasing space, be sure to take a look at the variety of shade and privacy options as well as ideas on ways to artfully accent your patio.

As its title suggests, Chapter 6, "Amenities," highlights bringing indoor comforts—such as showers and hearths—outside and discusses how to adapt these luxuries to their new setting. Plumbing and electricity issues are addressed so you can establish the foundation for outdoor kitchens, spas and pools, or whatever else your heart desires. Also explore ways to create visually appealing yet accessible paths and walkways that connect your outdoor spaces.

Providing an essential outdoor touch, plant life ties your deck and patio areas together with rich color and texture. In Chapter 7, "Incorporate Landscaping," you'll discover how to assess your landscaping needs and integrate landscaping into your deck or patio design.

The eyecatching options in Chapter 8, "Furnish the Space," show you how to successfully use colors, textures, outdoor furniture, fabrics, and accessories to transform your deck or patio into a visual treat.

As you move on to Chapter 9, "Final Considerations," use the project timeline and completion checklist to ensure that every step of the building process runs smoothly. Gather final inspiration from the case studies of three distinct outdoor spaces, which prove that you can create the outdoor retreat that fulfills your needs.

Chapter 10, "Resources," provides you with the names and contact information for some of the organizations and associations involved in deck and patio design projects. Brush up on the definitions of helpful terms you'll need when talking with professionals about your outdoor project.

Ready to get started?

CHAPTER 1

Explore Your Options

Outdoor Entertaining, Quiet Retreats, Poolside Fun,
Alfresco Dining, Family Gatherings, Styles & Themes

The first step in planning your outdoor space is certainly one of the most fun. It involves envisioning all the things you want your new outdoor area to be. Will you entertain large groups of people at evening dinner parties under the stars or curl up with a good book in a private, shaded nook on a lazy afternoon—or both? What will the outdoor space look like? Will it be a simple platform deck, a magnificent patio with multiple tiers, or an intimate perch overlooking spectacular views? At this point your options for expanding your outdoor living spaces are endless. Dare to dream now—pointers on how to revise that wish list to fit your budget are detailed later in this book.

This chapter features outstanding sites designed for entertaining, escaping, playing, dining, gathering, and more. Tour the featured locations then rely on your imagination to determine the deck or patio—or combination—that you want.

Swaying in the breeze, a chandelier creates glowing ambience for a small dinner party on this enclosed patio. Gauzy drapes are pulled back for sheer elegance.

OUTDOOR ENTERTAINING

Whether you're hosting a lively backyard barbecue or an intimate party for close friends, outdoor rooms offer an ideal spot to gather. To ensure you have an outdoor space that's up to the task of accommodating your guests, consider the types of events you'll host most frequently. Large parties will benefit from multiple outdoor rooms—perhaps a multilevel deck surrounded by several patios that transition to the yard beyond. Conversation will be livelier when guests can move from area to area. Multiple outdoor spaces provide the flexibility of having one area dedicated to a buffet table, another for grilling, yet another space for beverages, and still others for eating and conversation. If small gatherings are more your style, design outdoor spaces that help facilitate quiet conversation with good friends. Small groups will feel more intimate if the deck or patio is a modest size with furniture grouped for conversation.

Bringing Indoor Amenities Out

Heating and sound systems made for outdoor use extend the enjoyment of your outdoor space.

Heating keeps your outdoor room comfortable late into the evening or when the weather cools. To add warmth purchase weatherproof electric, infrared, or natural gas heaters that can be mounted or placed on the ground. Make sure your space is properly ventilated if you purchase a ventless gas heater.

Sound systems allow soft music to enhance your gatherings. Look for weatherproof models that are battery-operated or that can be plugged into a power conditioner so they're safe from surges. For even sound coverage strategically mount speakers above seating areas.

Simple touches transform an outdoor space into an inviting room. This weatherproof, shade cloth-covered pergola offers protection from the sun for daytime entertaining.

Colorful accents instantly enliven alfresco dining. Make a bold statement with candles, cut flowers, and vibrant table settings. Even fresh fruit lends an inexpensive splash of color.

DESIGN GALLERY
Entertaining Spaces

Few things say "welcome" quite like an outdoor space dressed in bold colors and rich textures. Look to these alluring rooms for inspiration when creating your inviting alfresco entertaining area.

1

2

1: Look for inventive ways to use your existing garden furnishings. Home to planting supplies, this potting bench also functions as a wet bar.

2: A small space offers an opportunity for close-knit gatherings that's too good to pass up. This seating arrangement is enhanced with Moroccan-inspired fabrics that infuse the space with warmth.

3: White lattice provides privacy for a deck dining party. The black and white umbrella supplies shade on hot days and continues the deck's color scheme.

4: A fiesta of colors brightens this functional outdoor kitchen that includes an island perfect for grabbing a quick bite. A ceiling fan circulates cool air throughout the space.

5: This spacious breezeway is ideal for hosting large gatherings, but the country French design scheme—defined by climbing vines and rustic decor—lends a more intimate feel.

QUIET RETREATS

You don't need much to have a spot well suited for reading the paper and sipping a cup of coffee in the morning or unwinding after work. Almost any small outdoor space will do. Transform an unused corner of a patio or deck into a place for quiet reflection with a comfortable chair and a few of your favorite things. Take a cue from the spaces featured. One is tucked close to the house and nestled amid potted plants and a bubbling fountain. Another features a cafe table for tea and chaise longues perfect for napping in the fresh air. If you're fortunate to have a secluded spot in the yard, design a patio or deck to take advantage of the solitude.

Nestled among a dense screen of plants, cozy seating invites solitude on this bluestone patio. The translucent railing encourages sunlight.

A pergola overlooking a restful reflecting pool defines an intimate space for dining and conversation, *left*. The waterfall provides soothing sounds.

Tucked in a quiet corner, this chaise longue is an ideal spot to curl up with a book, *right*. The freestanding fountain masks outside noises.

A peaceful, open space serves as a Zenlike retreat perfect for quiet reflection. The deck floats over a koi pond while surrounding trees offer a natural canopy to shield sunlight.

1

DESIGN GALLERY
Spots for Solitude

Set among the serene beauty of nature, the best seat in the house is actually located outdoors. These tranquil spaces offer a quiet, intimate escape for one or two.

1: This pair of rustic-look wooden chaise longues tucked beneath a deck create a hidden retreat surrounded by colorful desert-inspired scenery.

2: Deep burgundy and white flowers pop behind cream-color wicker chairs, soft blue cushions, and a black wrought-iron glass-top table.

3: A venue for relaxation requires only a small slice of deck as this cozy retreat proves. Two chairs surrounded by a bounty of blooms present an ideal afternoon getaway right at home.

4: A brick pavilion creates structure around this seating area without closing it off from the surrounding scenery. The warm hues of the bricks and wicker seating contrast with the cool gray slate patio tiles.

5: Framed by bougainvillea vines this English-style patio area provides a charming space for enjoying afternoon company and a glass of lemonade. The saltillo tiles add a Southwestern touch.

2

The unique T-shape pool and adjacent
whirlpool serve as the focal point in this yard.
A sloped roof extends over the large patio providing
shade for comfortable poolside lounging.

POOLSIDE FUN

Pools are natural gathering places in the summer. While the water certainly has appeal when temperatures soar be sure to think beyond the pool to the surrounding area as well. Much of the fun of a pool is what happens around it: relaxing near the water without leaving the comforts of your yard and home, watching the kids splash on a hot afternoon, and enjoying a lazy evening after a busy day of swimming. As with any outdoor room, consider your needs as you develop a plan for the best poolside deck, patio, or combination for your family. Expansive decking right up to the pool accommodates kids who will jump in and out of the water for much of the day. Include a shaded area nearby for adults to supervise without getting wet. If your pool will see more use from adults swimming laps or taking a quick, cooling dip, consider a narrow swath of decking adjacent to the pool coupled with a deck or patio with furnishings suitable for outdoor dining and conversation.

It's easy to host a pool party with several large tables scattered across the patio, *above*. The pergola and patio umbrellas above each table establish a sense of shelter from the midafternoon sun.

Housed in warm, desert-hue containers, tropical plants of varying heights create instant drama especially when paired with the neutral patio around this asymmetrical pool.

21

DESIGN GALLERY
Pool Views

Distinguished by soothing, crystal-clear water, these swimming pools beckon. But it's what you do with the area around the pool that truly adds impact. Dive into cool poolside design with these ideas.

1

1: Pool water cascades over a granite retaining wall into another narrow pool below. Boulders and the surrounding multilevel deck create visual interest.

2: Ample seating that accommodates friendly gatherings and personal space gives this poolside patio a relaxed atmosphere. For added comfort look for cushions made from weatherproof fabric.

3: A red, white, and blue color scheme brings a patriotic vibe to this pool. Colorful container plantings flank the stone patio that borders the pool.

4: Punctuated by bountiful plants, rustic materials such as stucco and weathered brick, and cozy furnishings, this peaceful setting resembles a Mediterranean-style villa.

5: An open garden room allows for poolside dining with unobstructed views. A plastic mesh ceiling creates welcome shade beneath the shelter on hot days.

2

ALFRESCO DINING

Your plans for an outdoor dining area should account for two basic requirements: cooking and eating. If cooking will be done indoors and food brought out for consumption, situate the outdoor dining space as close to the indoor kitchen as possible with a door to allow traffic to pass directly between the two areas. If you'll be cooking outdoors, consider what you'll fix, how frequently, and for how many people. A simple grill should suffice for family meals of burgers and hot dogs. The more elaborate your culinary endeavors, the more elaborate your outdoor kitchen. If multiple meals will be prepared and eaten outside each week, a full-service outdoor kitchen may be in order. Comfortable outdoor dining space requires a sturdy, level base so the table and chairs don't wobble. Allow sufficient space for a table large enough to seat the typical number of dinner guests.

A hidden set of stairs leads to an intricate circular brick pathway that's the perfect size for a dining table. The surrounding plants create natural privacy.

Design Tip

Want to add subtle flair to your outdoor dining space? Use patterned fabrics. Opt for large patterns in soft colors and detailed patterns in bolder hues. To create an attractive, layered look, set a short solid-color tablecloth on top of a patterned table skirt or vice versa. For more style bring out patterned pillows.

Dressed in rich colors and textures, this table sets the stage for an elegant alfresco dining experience. A built-in fireplace and candles add ambience.

An outdoor grill with an adjacent countertop makes food prep easy. This grill's neutral surround blends well with the scenery by mixing function with flair.

DESIGN GALLERY
Outdoor Dining

Enhanced by fresh breezes and breathtaking views, outdoor areas are idyllic backdrops for dining with family and friends. Here's how to add flavor to the setting of your next alfresco meal.

1: This table for two offers an intimate setting for conversation. Tall, upright plants dress a sloped wood retaining wall to create privacy while black river rock insets contrast with Irish linen stone pavers to add variety to the patio.

2: Turn an everyday meal into a festive occasion with beautiful table settings. The striking floral centerpiece rises to the occasion while pillar candles generate glowing ambience.

3: A multilevel deck provides ample space for large gatherings. Small tables positioned on each level create visual interest, and clusters of container plantings add a burst of color.

4: A wide umbrella shades this table from the warm sun to allow for daytime dining. Patio umbrellas come in a variety of styles to fit your needs.

5: Designed exclusively for dining this cozy framed deck sized perfectly for a single table encourages family togetherness.

3

4

5

This portable fire pit adds functionality and atmosphere for entertaining. Place your fire pit in a safe spot that's enjoyable for you but doesn't bother the neighbors.

FAMILY GATHERINGS

Get the entire family involved as you design an outdoor space that will meet the needs of everyone in your household. Ideally family spaces include a series of outdoor rooms with plenty of level space for young children's play, a spot for eating during casual summer cookouts, a seating area for teens to hang out with family and friends, and another space for the grown-ups to relax and supervise. A fireplace or fire pit offers a natural gathering spot. The one featured *opposite* is the focal point for a seating area large enough for the whole family to gather to roast marshmallows. A dining set on a larger wood deck is conveniently located off the kitchen and steps from the patio and fire pit.

This deck designed to please young children contains a sandbox. When playtime is over a hinged lid covers the sand and expands the deck surface area.

Design Tip

When installing a fire pit, make safety your priority. Situate the fire pit in an open area that's at least 10 feet from your house and 3 feet from outdoor furniture and other combustibles. Avoid areas near dry grass or leaves. Use a screen to prevent escaping sparks and be sure you always have a fire extinguisher or garden hose nearby.

DESIGN GALLERY
Fun Flourishes

Enhance the livability of your outdoor spaces with unexpected additions that encourage fun times with family and friends while infusing your deck or patio with character.

1: Leave a croquet set on your patio so guests can pick up mallets anytime they want to play. Casually propped against furniture these vintage croquet pieces add a subtle splash of color to the patio.

2: Drenched in vibrant hues a rustic wood table and chairs become the focal point of an outdoor kitchen. To personalize your outdoor living space, add pieces that reflect your style.

3: Incorporating an oversize game board in a garden adds instant whimsy. This checkerboard was handcrafted from inexpensive supplies found at a home improvement center.

4: A multilevel deck and patio combination provides plenty of places for kids to play while adults prepare dinner or relax.

5: This outdoor area has it all—hot tub, pool, fireplace, seating, and a swath of grass for running around—in one spot.

STYLES & THEMES

If you're looking for a starting point to determine the style of your outdoor living spaces, look no farther than your house. You can't go wrong when you give your deck or patio a look that complements its architecture. To achieve a simple and serene outdoor area, use slate, colored concrete, or concrete tiles. Choose subdued colors for large surfaces then add color with furnishings and accessories. Traditional homes tend to look best paired with flagstone or brick patios and decks with railings that mimic trimwork used on the home's exterior.

Regional styles may influence your design. Selecting local materials will help harmonize outdoor areas with your home's surroundings. They fit in best from a design perspective and probably will also be cost-effective.

The clean lines and simple shapes of this deck work with the fluid lines of the fence to establish a serene atmosphere. Plantings ease the transition between the deck and the koi pond. The overall effect is a tranquil backyard retreat.

Transform a small space into an inviting area with rich colors and textures. This urban dwelling boasts an assortment of container plantings, a small prayer rug, and comfortable seating with embellished pillows.

Overhead Styles

Overhead structures provide style and shade, but the key is to choose one that suits your outdoor space and complements the style of your home.

Create a rustic look by fashioning a pergola from all-natural materials such as twigs and limbs. Bentwood works especially well for the base. To protect your pergola from the weather, be sure to coat it with linseed oil.

Warm a contemporary home with a "nature-meets-modern" overhead structure made from wood and steel. For added flair match steel supports with steel and cable railings.

Play up a country or cottage garden theme with an all-white lattice structure. The white hue evokes country character while the latticework allows for good air circulation.

Defined by its generous use of cobalt blue Mexican Talavera and terra-cotta tiles, this outdoor room echoes the home's Spanish-style architecture.

A fresh coat of white paint can make a space pop as this outdoor pavilion proves. The classic color instills a sense of formality through the landscape.

CHAPTER 2

Plan the Project

*Determine Your Needs, Plan with a Purpose, Develop a Budget,
Hiring Professionals, Bids & Contracts,
Hiring a Contractor, Should You Do It Yourself?*

Once you've developed a basic idea of what you want, it's time to make the leap from dream to reality. This chapter will help you pinpoint the specific needs you want your deck or patio to fulfill and develop an action plan that will guide you through the rest of the project. You'll want to tackle the specifics up front: Set a budget that's manageable and determine whether you'll need to hire professionals. As you peruse this chapter, you'll find essential information about bids, estimates, and contracts to help you form a positive working relationship with contractors.

DETERMINE YOUR NEEDS

Before you think about location, size, shape, or materials for your new outdoor living space, decide how you want to use it. Determining its function will help you make the right choices going forward. Answer these questions to get started.

How much time will you spend in an outdoor room?

What will you do there? For multiple uses a series of rooms may be more effective than one large space.

Who will be there with you? If you regularly entertain large groups, you'll need more space than if you want a quiet spot for two.

What makes a comfortable outdoor environment for you? If insects drive you crazy but you crave fresh air, a screen porch may be essential. If you're always chilly the warmth of a fireplace may extend the months your outdoor spaces are in use.

Will your needs change in the near future? The needs of a young, growing family may shift rapidly. While it's important to plan a space that works well now, the added expense of overhauling a new deck or patio in a couple of years may be much higher than adding features now that will make the space work long into the future.

A stately brick fireplace warms cool-weather outdoor gatherings while a built-in flat-panel LCD TV provides entertainment. The TV is protected by a weatherproof cabinet when not in use.

Complete with a full-service kitchen and media options, this waterfront deck includes ample amenities to keep a crew happy outdoors for an entire day.

A series of outdoor spaces—such as this multilevel patio and second-floor deck— may suit the needs of your family better than a single outdoor room.

A privacy fence encloses this brick patio, creating solitude for dining or relaxing. Smart planning ensures even placement of the patio bricks so the table and chairs won't wobble when in use.

PLAN WITH A PURPOSE

Transforming an outdoor living space from dream to reality often is simpler than interior remodeling projects because most of the mess stays outside. Though the end result will enhance your home and lifestyle, a patio or deck isn't quite the essential space a kitchen or a bathroom is. But having a plan for the process helps. Keep your focus on the function of the new deck or patio. This will help you choose the best materials; determine the optimum size, shape, and location; decide on amenities; select furnishings; and address any maintenance required of your selections.

Enjoy the visual feast of patios and decks in this book. Consider how each might meet your needs and integrate with your house, lifestyle, and budget. Also take note of components of spaces you like. Even if the overall design wouldn't work for you, could elements be integrated into your plan? Visit local landscape stores. Most have elaborate displays that showcase materials readily available in your area, and many will have portfolios of recent projects so you can gather more ideas and evaluate potential contractors for your project. Finally, start refining your choices. Eliminating materials, amenities, and structures that won't fit your budget allows you to focus on what you can achieve. And that's what will make your new outdoor room a reality.

Consider which materials—from wood decking to brick—will work best with the style and location of your outdoor space before making any final decisions.

A rustic-look flagstone path and an abundance of pretty flowers easily transform the area surrounding this deck into a cottage-style retreat that blooms with vibrant hues.

DEVELOP A BUDGET

As with almost everything in life, setting a budget for your new outdoor living spaces probably will involve some compromises. Start by deciding how much you can afford to spend. Outdoor rooms are just that—living spaces on the exterior of your home. As a result they may be very costly, depending on the size, materials, amenities, and particulars of your location. Knowing what you can spend should make it easier to determine which features you can include now and which will have

to be added later. Involve the entire family in making a list of everything you'd like from your new deck or patio. Then divide your list into two parts: one for everything you need to have and the second for everything you want to have. As you talk with professionals and get bids for the project, you'll be able to determine how many of your desires are within your budget. Remember to add a 5 to 10 percent cushion to estimates and bids to account for cost overruns and changes in plans.

Simple additions can yield elegant results. A wrought-iron pergola, *left*, covered with climbing roses, clematis, and akebia enhances alfresco dining.

Crabapple trees and yews create inexpensive yet attractive privacy for this brick dining terrace, *above*. Remember to consider how much landscaping—like the formal perennial garden beyond this patio—will cost.

Natural sandstone interspersed with budget-friendly precast cobblestones paves this secluded courtyard, *right*. Dwarf shrubs keep the floor plan open while decorative planters soften the shady dining nook.

HIRING PROFESSIONALS

Though in their simplest form patios and decks are fairly basic structures, more elaborate designs and construction are becoming the norm as more people desire to spend leisure time enjoying the comforts of home. If your ideas for an outdoor living space go beyond builder-basic, consult a design professional. Working with a design professional helps ensure the items on your wish list become reality. Professionals' experience enables them to develop creative solutions to potential problems, meet code requirements, and recommend cost-effective ways to achieve your goals. If the cost of hiring professionals seems prohibitive, consider that their knowledge may help you avoid costly mistakes. They also can contribute to project efficiencies by organizing and managing the project, which may ultimately result in lower project costs.

Three types of design professionals typically work on a deck or patio project. Although they have specialized areas of expertise, most professionals are well-versed in all phases of design and can help create a comprehensive plan.

Architects work primarily with structure and reorganization of space. They are familiar with many types of building materials, finishes, and structural systems. Architects are a good choice for complex deck designs because they will design your deck and make sure it is sensibly integrated with adjacent living areas such as your kitchen or family room. Architects charge a percentage of the project's total cost—usually 10 to 15 percent—or work on an hourly basis.

Landscape architects registered with the American Society of Landscape Architects (ASLA) are usually designers only; the plans they furnish must be given to a landscape contractor for final installation. Occasionally a professional landscape architect joins with a landscape contractor to offer full-service planning and installation. An ASLA architect typically charges hourly fees to analyze your property and complete detailed drawings that recommend plantings and landscape features to help connect your new space to its outdoor environment. Expect to pay 15 percent of the cost of the finished landscape project for a landscape plan.

Landscape contractors can install decks, patios, walkways, retaining walls, plantings, and ancillary structures such as pergolas and arbors. Many landscape contractors are full-service firms that have landscape architects, designers, and installers and can provide a range of services that include initial concepts, finalized plans, installation, and ongoing maintenance.

Hire a landscape architect to design an outdoor space that blossoms with visual interest. This patio floor and lily of the Nile flowers draw the eye when positioned against the gray-stained redwood fence, bench, and pergola.

An architect is an essential part of the project team for a two-story deck such as this one. The upper-level decking includes grates that allow light to filter into the lower level of the house.

Locate a Design Professional

Hiring a qualified professional is essential to creating a dream deck or patio so it's good to look around. To locate design professionals in your area, refer to your local phone book or search the websites of the American Society of Landscape Architects (www.asla.org) or the North American Deck and Railing Association (www.nadra.org).

These organizations are governed by codes of ethics to ensure fair working relationships. You can find the codes on the organizations' websites. Some sites also have industry information to help you stay updated on current trends. If experience is a major factor in your decision-making process, check with the organizations to determine the certification types they require of their members.

This raised deck coordinates with the architectural style of the house as well as incorporates materials and colors similar to the house. To ensure proper attention to such details request an itemized bid.

BIDS & CONTRACTS

Obtaining Bids

If you'll be hiring a contractor to build the deck or install the patio, you'll need to get a bid from each individual or firm you're considering. To make the bidding process most efficient, have a finalized project plan before requesting bids. Be sure to include specific materials in your plans. A concrete slab patio will cost significantly less than the same patio made of an uncommon flagstone, and a deck of pressure-treated lumber will cost much less than the same configuration made of ipe decking. The process of comparing bids will be simplified when you're able to compare apples to apples. Ask the contractors to submit itemized bids in person so you can discuss what is included and what is not.

Figuring Estimates

If you're doing the work yourself, an estimate of expenses will allow you to determine whether the project is within your budget. In addition to all materials, include costs for buying or renting tools you don't have. While it helps to shop around a bit for good prices, remember that your time is valuable. Spending too much time driving from store to store to buy the lowest-price supplies probably will cost you more than buying everything from one reasonably priced supplier.

Design Tip

No matter how carefully bids are prepared, savvy homeowners know that a deck or patio project can cost 10 to 15 percent more than estimated. Unexpected problems and changes are common. After the project is under way, it's easy for enthusiastic homeowners to get caught up in the process and want to upgrade plans and materials. Spare yourself the hassle and headaches by anticipating budget overruns from the beginning.

To achieve a beautifully designed and landscaped patio like this one, it's important to review several bids from contractors. Make sure all features, such as this intricate brick fountain, are included in the bids.

If you hire a professional to build your deck or patio, check that the contract contains information about every aspect of the job.

Making a Contract

If you decide to use a contractor, you'll need to sign a written contract after you've finalized your choice. The contract should include a:

- **Detailed description of all work** to be completed by the contractor and any responsibilities you'll handle.
- **Specific list of all materials** to be used in the project. If applicable the list should include brand, color, size, shape, finish, and plant varieties.
- **Rundown of the total cost** of the job.
- **Schedule of payments**. It is common to pay a portion up front to help cover the cost of materials, but the amount should be a small percentage. Remaining installments should be tied to work completed rather than to dates because weather and other extenuating circumstances will affect the schedule, and you shouldn't have to pay for work that has yet to be completed.
- **Tentative schedule for completion**. Schedules for outdoor projects may be affected by inclement weather, but the contract should provide a tentative start and finish date.
- **Certificate of insurance** that guarantees that the contractor has the appropriate coverage.
- **Warranty** that guarantees that the labor and materials are free from defects for a certain period of time, usually one year.
- **Specific arbitration clause** listing the precise method you will use to settle any disputes.
- **Description of change-order procedures**, stating what will happen if you decide to alter the plans or specifications after the contract has been signed and a fee structure for how much any changes will cost.
- **Release of liens** to ensure that you won't incur liens or charges against your property as a result of legal actions filed against the contractor or subcontractors.

Comparing Bids

When it's time to evaluate bids:

Check that each contractor has the same information about your project. Otherwise prices may vary because components won't be consistent with all the bids.

Compare line items from bid to bid. One estimate for materials may be less than another because the materials are lower quality. Consider whether budget or quality is more important to you.

Watch out for extremely low bids. The bid could be low because it doesn't include all aspects of the job.

Base your decision on more than the final cost. Compare the estimated time frame between bids—higher costs are justified if the work is being done on a faster schedule. Check with references from each contractor and factor them into your decision.

Ask the contractor to clarify or further explain if you don't understand an estimate on the bid before you make a decision.

No matter how large or small the project is, make sure your contract contains a precise list of materials.

Integrating budget-friendly materials into most of your project allows you to splurge on a few luxurious items such as these striking cobalt blue mosaic tiles.

A contractor can help you construct a deck or patio that fits the style and structure of your home.

HIRING A CONTRACTOR

Decks and patios can be relatively easy to complete compared with many other home improvement projects, but they require skills (and muscles) that you may rarely use and tools you may not have. If time for the project is limited to evenings and weekends, you may spend more time building the project than enjoying it. In cases such as these, it's smart to hire a contractor. Take the time necessary to choose a contractor who has a good reputation and with whom you feel comfortable. To find a qualified general contractor:

- **Ask friends,** neighbors, or colleagues for the names of reliable contractors they have hired. Get several recommendations.
- **Meet with prospective contractors** to discuss your project. Ask about their experience with deck or patio projects similar to yours. Ask for a ballpark figure for the project.
- **Ask how long** they have been in business and whether they carry insurance. Without insurance you're liable for accidents that occur on your property.
- **Obtain references** from contractors and take the time to inquire about and, if possible, inspect their work.

Detailed projects such as this elaborate garden shed demand a lot of time and materials. Be sure to hire a contractor who has the experience to create exactly what you want.

Working With a Contractor

To achieve the best results, you'll want a good working relationship with your contractor. Keep these tips in mind for easy completion of your deck or patio project.

Check in frequently. Although it may be unrealistic to be at home every time the contractor comes to work, try to coordinate a time every day to discuss the progress. That way you quickly can assess the work done the previous day and discuss any problems or upcoming decisions. Once you've met for a few minutes, avoid hovering.

Communicate. Speak up immediately if you are displeased about anything. The longer you wait the more expensive and difficult corrections will be. Be polite but clear about what you would rather see. Also remember to express what you're pleased with as the project moves along—compliments can go a long way.

Get changes in writing. Though you want to minimize costly changes, you may need to alter plans after work has started. Write out any "change work" agreements and make them as precise and detailed as the original contract.

Talk money. Before the project starts decide with your contractor how often you'll discuss money. Frequent checkpoints will allow you both to assess whether the project is on budget. Be prepared to discuss how setbacks might affect the budget and how you can adjust the plan to keep costs down.

Incorporating a water feature like this pond into your outdoor living space adds depth and serenity, but it's best to let someone with experience handle the installation.

SHOULD YOU DO IT YOURSELF?

If you're the type who gets just as much enjoyment from installing decking as you will sipping lemonade on the deck once the project is complete, you may be a good candidate to complete the project yourself. Installing a patio or building a deck is a fairly common do-it-yourself project. Before you break out the saw, screwdriver, and fasteners, however, consider everything that's involved and do an honest self-assessment.

Physical Labor

Depending on the scope of your plans, building a deck or installing a patio can be a huge physical undertaking. If you intend to do every step of the project yourself, you'll need to purchase all the materials, load them into a vehicle that can withstand their weight, transport them to your house, unload them, and move them to the site. All that and construction hasn't even begun. Digging footings, mixing concrete, clearing a site large enough for a patio, moving heavy flagstones—all are strenuous activities.

Cost

If your only rationale for doing the work yourself is a vision of dollars saved, remember the potential costs associated with undertaking the project yourself. Though you won't need many specialized tools for a deck or patio, if this is your first home improvement project, you may spend a bundle purchasing essential tools such as a circular saw, mitersaw, level, and square. If you realistically expect this is the first of many projects you'll tackle yourself, the purchases will be good investments. If, however, this is the only project you'll do, the costs likely will offset any savings. You may also have to rent a vehicle to transport the materials to your home. Materials for a patio, in particular, are extremely heavy and far exceed the load limits for most standard vehicles. And lumber typically fits in only the largest of trucks. Finally contractors typically receive discounts on materials because they purchase in greater volume—that's a savings you won't receive when you're purchasing small quantities.

Time

What in reality is a small patio may seem as if it engulfs the entire neighborhood when you're digging out sod to create the base, pouring and trying to level wheelbarrow after wheelbarrow of gravel, and attempting to piece together hundreds of bricks or flagstones. If your idea of fun is spending your weekends puttering around the house making improvements, then building a deck or patio qualifies as quality recreational time. If you long to relax on the new outdoor area, however, the time commitment—especially if you can work on the project only at night and on the weekends—may seem overwhelming.

Safety

Though building a deck or patio is not the most hazardous of home improvement projects, there are safety considerations. Building a deck involves saws, nails, screws, and other items that require safe techniques and handling as well as appropriate safety gear. If you have children or pets, the job site will need to be secured. If you plan to work on the project after spending all day at your full-time job, fatigue may affect your safety. You need to be alert and cautious while operating power tools.

Overhead structures like pergolas don't require many materials and can be inexpensive to build.

Design Tip

Even if you hire professional help to tackle the bulk of your deck or patio building project, you can save money by doing certain tasks yourself. Clear the site of trees, plants, or anything else that's not worth saving before construction begins. Volunteer to clean the construction site at the end of each day. Paint or finish your deck or patio after it's built. Or even build basic structures such as a pergola or planters.

To build a patio as spacious as this, it may be best to enlist a contractor's expertise. If you're determined to tackle a large project yourself, complete it in sections.

CHAPTER 3

Evaluate the Site

Site Evaluation, Property Shape, Slope, Shade, Views, Develop a Site Map,
Incorporate Existing Landscaping, Create Visual Harmony,
Access & Traffic Flow, Building Code Requirements

Before you begin building your dream deck or patio, critically examine what you're working with by taking into account the shape and size of your property. At times your property may hinder your plans, but with a little creativity you can turn these problems into assets. Explore information about creating shade, making the most of great views, and seamlessly connecting your outdoor living space to your house and existing landscape. To visualize your plans create a site map that shows all of the essential elements of your deck and patio design. Finally, with your desired layout in mind, read about building code requirements—a safe and compliant deck should be your top priority.

SITE EVALUATION

Decks and patios provide a transition between your home's interior rooms and the yard beyond the house. When well planned they function as outdoor rooms and as part of the landscape. Take advantage of the ability of a well-designed deck or patio to improve your house and yard. At first glance a steeply sloped yard may offer little or no usable space. But with some thoughtful planning, you may discover that using your backyard is as easy as building a raised deck or a series of tiered patios that nestle into the slope.

Spend some time in your yard during the planning stages. What works in your neighbor's yard won't necessarily be the right solution in yours. Creating an outdoor living area that integrates the best attributes of your property and overcomes the worst should be a primary goal.

If one section of your yard is more level than the rest, take a cue from this patio and create a private outdoor room surrounded by a fence. Using the same fencing material throughout the backyard keeps the look consistent.

Native plants and stonework provide a seamless transition from this home to the swimming pool.

To break up the height between the home's upper-level enclosed deck and the lawn, this yard boasts a limestone retaining wall. The circular dining patio takes advantage of the tree-shaded lot.

Cohesive Outdoor Rooms

When you have multiple outdoor rooms, it's important to establish unity throughout each space to avoid a jarring look. Here's how:

Color consistency. Stick to the same color scheme used for the exterior of your house and weave that color palette throughout each room. To give each space a similar yet distinctive look, experiment with color intensity.

Minimal materials. Use the same flooring material in each room to create visual flow. Also incorporate similar surface materials such as lattice walls, fencing, or plantings throughout.

Distinct decor. Look to your home's exterior for inspiration when adding details. For example, if your home is heavy on copper fixtures, add touches of copper to your outdoor rooms. If your front porch is home to terra-cotta planters, continue the look in the backyard.

PROPERTY SHAPE

No matter the shape of your property, take it into consideration when you select the location and design of your deck or patio. A small, narrow, or unusually shaped yard may present the most design restrictions. Yet these characteristics also can simplify the planning process so you can focus on selecting materials, furnishings, and amenities. And while a large property is likely to afford many options in regard to the location, size, and shape of a deck or patio, you may be overwhelmed by your choices. Designing a deck or patio that contrasts with your property's shape may visually enhance the landscape. If you live in a neighborhood of square lots, for example, a curved deck or patio can break the monotony of all the straight lines. No matter what your property offers, there is certain to be a workable solution for an outdoor living space that meets your family's needs.

This spacious brick patio avoids a flat, one-dimensional look with tiered levels and raised flowerbeds. The purple plantings are a pleasant contrast against the warm terra-cotta brick tones.

A diminutive octagon-shape deck allows enough room for this intimate seating arrangement that takes advantage of surrounding mature blooming plants.

Property Easements

Easements are corridors on your property that must be kept free of structures. If your planned deck or patio is near property lines or your property borders a public park, it's important to check for:

- **Utility** easements that allow access to utilities to make repairs. They are often at the back of a property.

- **Overland** flow easements including gullies that collect water during heavy rains. They cannot be altered or blocked by construction.

- **Accessibility** easements that ensure there's enough space for a driveway so you can access a road from your house if a property has been split into a front and back parcel.

- **Buffer** easements that protect parks adjacent to your property.

A stimulating medley of colors and textures makes the most of this narrow courtyard. Layered shrubs and perennials produce a pretty palette every growing season. The stone pathway design minimizes the need for lawn care.

SLOPE

If your yard is modestly—or even steeply—sloped, a deck or series of patios can help render it a more usable space. A raised deck, for example, can be vaulted over changes in terrain. A cantilevered deck that extends beyond the support structures underneath it is particularly useful if the property drops off sharply beyond the house. If a patio is more your style, it may be possible to grade the soil into terraces with each one the site of a future patio space linked by a series of steps. If land slopes toward the house, drainage should be addressed before any work is done to the deck or patio. A good drainage system will carry runoff away from the foundation of the house. No matter the natural slope of the ground, a finished patio should provide a slight slope away from the house so water doesn't pool near the foundation and cause problems. A design professional will help you incorporate this slope into plans for the patio.

A raised deck looks out over a steep yard. Instead of being leveled to a flat surface, the slope was transformed into a visual treat with stacked stones and a tumbling waterfall.

This wraparound deck extends to the side yard on a sloped lot, providing a beautiful outdoor area in a spot that otherwise couldn't be used.

SHADE

You'll get the best use from a deck or patio that benefits from a balance of sun and shade. Except for the hottest part of the day, filtered shade is more comfortable than total shade or complete sun. Afternoon shade during the hottest months is ideal and typically is available on the east side of the house or under a large tree. If the deck or patio is tucked against your house, the house itself will provide some shade.

Create shade if your yard doesn't offer the natural variety. Overheads and screens provide relief from the sun and make stunning visual additions to an outdoor structure (see pages 94–97 and 134–135 for more information). Awnings that attach to and extend from the house are another convenient option for flexible shade. Extend the awning when the sunlight is too bright and close it for more light. And one of the easier options is to purchase a large table umbrella.

Keep in mind that shade structures don't always block the sun for people directly underneath them. During the late afternoon sunlight coming from a low angle won't be blocked or filtered without vertical screens.

The strategic placement of trees can ensure a shady retreat. A quartet of trees stand guard around this open patio to help filter sunlight.

Cool Canopies

These materials bring instant shade to your outdoor space:

Slatted wood and **lattice** allow filtered sunlight to subtly brighten your space. Another bonus: They offer privacy without a sense of confinement.

Bamboo provides a natural look. Store it inside during the winter and be sure to replace it after several seasons.

Canvas shields your space from sun and rain as long as you keep it sloped and taut.

Shade cloth allows dappled light and fresh breezes and comes in a variety of airy styles, but it isn't waterproof.

VIEWS

If you're lucky your yard already presents a breathtaking view—or at least a pleasing one. If so, orient your new deck or patio to take full advantage of the scenery. If you can watch the sun rise over the ocean or see it set behind the mountains, it's probably worth exposing your deck to harsh sunlight during the heat of the day for the pleasure of the spectacular morning or evening views. But less impressive displays also are worth consideration. Position your patio next to a perennial garden so you can view your gardening efforts and, if you have fragrant flowers, benefit from the scent as well. Think about children's play too. Parents of young children will feel more relaxed if the new deck is situated with a clear view of play structures, while parents of teens may want a private deck tucked outside the master bedroom. It's also important to think about views you should avoid. You may feel exposed rather than relaxed if nosy neighbors have an unhindered view of your new patio.

This Arts and Crafts-style deck captures a pristine view of the ocean. Cushioned lounge chairs add to the relaxing atmosphere.

A flat, open deck simply accented with plantings showcases an unobstructed spot from which to take in the sights and smells of the water.

DEVELOP A SITE MAP

If you've ever remodeled a kitchen or bathroom, you probably used some type of planning kit with templates of cabinetry and fixtures to plot the space before plans were finalized. Similar planning for a deck, patio, or series of outdoor rooms can be just as helpful to accomplishing your goals for the project. The backyard shown *opposite* includes a series of family-friendly outdoor rooms with a large deck for dining positioned off the kitchen, a lower patio with furnishings arranged for conversation, and a smaller deck off the master bedroom. Built-in benches line the upper deck and guarantee ample seating for parties. A trellis and arbor shield the view from neighbors without making the space seem walled-in. The multilevel, multifunctional space replaced a standard builder deck that had just enough room for a table and four chairs. To effectively use your outdoor spaces, a site map of some sort is almost essential. Just draw your property, the house, any existing hardscapes such as fences and walkways, and landscaping that will remain. Make several copies and then start sketching new outdoor living spaces. Once you have a basic design you like, check sizes of furnishings and other amenities to ensure that you have ample space for activities in addition to the items you plan to place on your deck or patio.

It may be helpful to determine the arrangement of smaller furnishings in advance. This location brims with furniture and planters, yet the floor plan remains fully accessible.

Drawing a site map is essential in creating a deck like this with three distinct yet connected zones that provide room for personal reflection and large gatherings.

A stone path winds its way to a circular patio defined by dense greenery. To give a formal-looking patio a touch of fun, use unusual objects—like wheelbarrows—as planters.

INCORPORATE EXISTING LANDSCAPING

Much of the enchantment of an outdoor room is the beauty that surrounds it. Fragrant flowers, colorful blooms, and trees that provide dappled shade all contribute to the relaxing atmosphere. If your landscape includes such features make sure to incorporate them into your new plans. If you are working with a design professional who specializes in landscaping, the designer will map existing trees, shrubs, and gardens and integrate them with your new deck or patio. Also be mindful of existing hardscapes that can enhance an outdoor room. If a path leads from the yard to the house, save at least part of the path so that it will lead from the new deck or patio into the yard, an approach that's sensible for traffic flow and your budget. Ripping out the old path and installing a new one would just add to the project costs.

This patio was created amid a serene garden setting. With an assortment of low-growing plants, medium-height shrubs, and stately trees, the landscaping boasts a layered look that makes the patio seem more spacious than it actually is.

Preserving Mature Trees

Though they provide shade and beauty, mature trees can stand in the way of your deck and patio design. Protect trees during the building process with these tips.

Talk with a professional arborist who can examine the trees on your property and help you determine a plan of action.

Build a patio or deck that contours around the tree and does not invade the tree's root system.

Install a fence around the tree to protect the root system during construction.

Avoid compacting soil around the tree—this inhibits root growth and decreases essential oxygen in the soil.

A cluster of containers planted with colorful flowers enlivens this plain deck. Potted plants are portable and easy to care for. Vary the heights of plants for eyecatching interest.

CREATE VISUAL HARMONY

Just as an addition should look like it has always been a part of the original house, so should a new deck or patio look as though it belongs with your home. Compatibility between your house and new outdoor living space will help establish visual harmony between the two structures. Consider the size and shape of the house, the materials used, and the scale and placement of stairs and railings.

Take cues from the existing house. Structural elements such as posts and railings should be thoughtfully selected and blend well with the overall design of the house. A low platform deck, for example, fits well with the shape and scale of a single-story ranch-style home. Such a simple deck design would be out of place attached to a larger, ornate Victorian house. For that you may want to add posts and railings that complement details from cornices or window trim and possibly paint it to match existing woodwork.

Avoid introducing new materials that are radically different from what already exists. A two-story brick home suggests using brick pavers rather than plain concrete. When you do mix textures and colors, tie them together. That plain concrete patio will look better if the concrete is tinted or stained to match the brick or if it is surrounded by a brick border.

Scale is important. Even if money is no object and you imagine the grandest of deck/patio combinations, the final design should be carefully scaled so that it is in proportion with your house.

Design Tip

A cohesive outdoor space should look like a natural extension of your home so use your home's architectural style for design inspiration. For example a grand, traditional home may call for a formal English outdoor room while a stucco dwelling might look best paired with a Southwestern-inspired patio.

The formal structure of the plantings and brickwork that edges this grassy walkway echoes the formality of the stately brick houses in the area.

This wooden walkway leads from the house to the adjacent garden. The flat wood platforms rest on the ground, offering a level walking surface.

Furnishings arranged on a deck or patio should be positioned clear of exterior doors that open outward so they don't block traffic flow.

ACCESS & TRAFFIC FLOW

The amount of use your new deck or patio gets is directly related to how easy it is to access—both from the inside of your home and from the rest of the yard. If it's difficult to get to the deck or patio, you probably won't use it much no matter how lovely the design and amenities. Where the new outdoor room connects to the house should be a matter of function. Position an outdoor dining area directly outside the kitchen with access through a door that opens into the kitchen. Family rooms are a logical transition point for accessing a general-use deck or patio. A private deck makes the most sense when located off the master bedroom.

Traffic flow also is critical. New doorway locations might make it easy to access the outdoor room but could affect furniture placement and how people move through an interior room. Interior flooring will be exposed to increased wear so select durable flooring that will withstand dirt and moisture and will be easy to clean. Plan traffic patterns through the outdoor space. Arrange furniture much as you would inside. Group furnishings for easy conversation. Position tables and furniture groupings away from natural traffic flow. If possible plan nooks for the grill in a spot close to the interior kitchen but out of the way of most outdoor activities.

BUILDING CODE REQUIREMENTS

Building codes might seem a hindrance on the path to making your plans a reality, but they are designed to ensure that new structures are safe and structurally sound. Any structure attached to the house requires a building permit before construction begins. Some freestanding structures may require permits as well. Permits are issued after a local building department has reviewed plans for your new structure.

Once construction is under way, a local building inspector probably will make several visits to examine the structure to ensure that it is being built safely and in compliance with local codes. When you apply for the building permit, ask at which stages the inspector will need to review the work. Make sure someone will be on-site to answer questions when the inspector visits.

A deck with detailed architecture, such as this structure with curved steps and stately pillars, requires specific and accurate building plans.

When you're planning an elaborate cooking center such as this, you'll want to ensure the placement of plumbing and electricity is approved before you begin.

If you're concerned about electrical safety issues such as how to conceal wiring, don't hesitate to ask the building inspector.

Before adding decorative structures like these wooden planters, it's important to check that they're well-mounted so they don't fall.

Even the most basic deck designs may need approval. Railings and stairs commonly require approval.

DESIGN GALLERY
Stunning Sites

Sometimes it's not the shape or size of your site that matters, it's what you do with it. Take cues from these locations and transform your property into a site to behold with smart material selections.

1: A spacious, open property leaves plenty of room for this formal patio. The symmetrical design is achieved with clipped boxwood hedges, straight brick paths, and a center fountain.

2: Subtly nestled against a curved retaining wall, this bistro table allows people to take advantage of the mature oak trees and unusual plants that surround this patio.

3: Small spaces can be transformed into attractive retreats with colorful low-growing plants as this deck proves.

4: Topped by a Craftsman-style arbor, this double-foursquare fence invites solitude. The close-growing plants around the fence enhance privacy.

5: Wood decking that features brick borders and raised brick planters forms an attractive seating area that nestles into the edge of this property. The fence and tiered plantings create a comfortable backdrop.

CHAPTER 4

Deck Basics

Deck Configurations, Deck Construction, Decking, Decking Patterns, Fasteners, Railings, Stairs & Ramps, Skirting & Screens, Overhead Structures, Built-Ins, Finishing & Maintenance

Building a deck helps infuse your property with structural integrity. During the process many important choices will arise, and the deck terminology in this chapter will give you the know-how to make informed decisions. Explore the variety of decking options to create a stylish and sturdy structure. Also examine deck components such as railings, stairs and ramps, skirting and screens, overheads, and built-ins that provide structural support and opportunities for customization. When you have all the pieces of your deck put together, apply a good-quality finish and take other measures to protect it from wear and tear. Then all that's left to do is enjoy it.

DECK CONFIGURATIONS

How you want to use your new deck and the size, shape, and contour of your yard have the biggest impacts on the type of deck. To accommodate the increasing popularity of outdoor living, decks rapidly are becoming larger and grander. You may determine, however, that a small deck will best fit your yard and lifestyle.

Multilevel decks are in high demand. These structures add visual interest and break up a landscape. They're particularly good for sloped yards and can enhance a too-plain flat yard. Multilevel decks and raised decks provide bonus space under the deck structure. Put this space to good use by adding storage containers, shelves, and hooks to stow lawn and garden equipment. Or double your outdoor living opportunities by tucking another outdoor room under the deck. See the sidebar *opposite* for more ideas on putting underdeck space to work. If you have a yard smaller than 500 square feet, however, a small, single-level structure may be a better fit.

A stately raised deck breaks up the height of this three-story home. The minimal number of support beams creates additional play space underneath.

Small in size this platform deck, *above,* stays proportionate to the rest of the house and creates a sense of unity. Traffic easily flows from indoors out.

This multilevel deck, *below,* boasts several rooms to accommodate the whole family. Two arbors with overhead lattice establish privacy and filter sunlight.

Using Space Under a Raised Deck

The empty space beneath your raised deck is too good to pass up: The deck provides a fully covered roof, and you can add further definition with screens along the sides that allow filtered sunlight and fresh breezes to circulate. Add inconspicuous deck lighting to the support posts, and you have a fully functional space. Consider turning yours into:

Storage space. Corral occasional-use items beneath your deck to avoid clutter above while keeping them easily accessible. Install side screens to help protect items from the weather; build shelves for even more organization.

Outdoor rooms. Expand your outdoor living potential by arranging furnishings to create another outdoor room. Another bonus: Because the space underneath is defined by the deck's structural supports, it will be easy to maintain a cohesive look. For added style echo the color, decor, and surface materials used above.

A basic platform deck benefits from a dose of style with a painted overhead structure that resembles a home's roof. The overhead lends a sense of shelter and dimension to the flat deck.

Curved decks are another popular trend because of their shape. They're ideal for adding built-in benches and other architectural details.

Platform decks are the simplest style. When built low to the ground, they often don't require railings and thus make excellent transition spaces between the house and yard. String together a series of platform decks for impact.

Raised decks are ideal if you have a walkout lower level and want outdoor space that extends from the upper portion of the house. Plan for stairs that make it easy and safe to access the yard. As with a multilevel deck, consider uses for the space under the deck. Because the structural support system of a raised deck is exposed, use foundation plantings or skirting to conceal the structure if you won't otherwise use the space underneath.

Freestanding decks offer great flexibility because the structure is not attached to the house. Place a freestanding deck away from your home to take advantage of the best views, a shady stand of trees, or a blooming garden.

Design Tip

To prevent water seepage between deck boards, line the top of existing boards with vinyl membrane sheeting or look for deck drainage systems that channel rainwater into a gutter. Also consider deck systems with interlocking panels.

These support structures, *left*, boast curved lattice detailing for unexpected visual interest. The decorative details blend with the home's architectural style.

This distinctive freestanding deck wraps around a water garden. A backdrop of mature trees and a covered bench shelter the deck and lend the comfortable feel of an outdoor room with walls.

DECK CONSTRUCTION

Decks are basic structures, but the final design can be complex. Becoming familiar with the terms used in deck construction will make planning your deck, ordering materials, and overseeing any changes to plans easier. Understanding deck terminology helps you communicate effectively with designers, builders, and other contractors.

Multilevel decks require more complex structures than platform decks. Because they are not hidden from view as other portions of the deck substructure are, the posts that support the top-level sunroom here are finished to look like decorative columns.

Deck Substructures

A deck has two types of components. The supporting portion of a deck, called the substructure, is typically hidden from view beneath the deck. Wood used to make the substructure must be strong, durable lumber such as pressure-treated wood, which combines strength and moisture resistance for a reasonable cost.

- **Footings** are cylinders of poured concrete that extend into the ground and support individual posts. Building codes require that they extend below the frost line. This prevents the seasonal cycles of freezing and thawing from disturbing the position of the footings over the years. A footing usually is 36 to 42 inches deep. The location of the footings depends on the size and shape of the deck.

- **Pier blocks** (not illustrated) are set on top of the footings while the footing concrete is still wet. Made of precast concrete and about 8 inches on each side, they elevate the posts to keep them from coming into contact with the ground, preventing moisture damage. Some pier blocks include metal hardware for a secure connection to posts.

- **Posts** extend up from the footings and form the vertical supports of a deck. The thickness of the posts depends on the configuration of the deck structure. Thicker posts spaced farther apart can take the place of thinner posts that are closer together. Posts should be made of pressure-treated lumber to prevent rot and insect attacks. Tall posts—such as those required for second-story decks—need angled supports called bracing to provide stability.

- **Joists** form a grid for supporting the decking material. Often called "two-by" lumber, joists are 1½ inches thick and are installed on edge. The sizes of the joists are determined by the span of the deck: The longer the span the heftier the joist. Joists at the perimeter of a deck are called end joists. End joists usually are doubled to provide firm support around the deck edges.

- **Beams,** or girders, are large pieces of lumber used to support joists. The beams are attached to the posts and run at right angles to the joists. Depending on the size and configuration of a deck, beams may not be necessary. Like all structural components, beams made from pressure-treated lumber combine strength and durability.

- **Ledger board** is a joist mounted against the side of a house to provide support for one side of a deck. The ledger board is bolted or screwed to the house; the space behind the ledger is sealed with caulk and covered with flashing to prevent water from penetrating the house. Joists usually are attached to the ledger with joist hangers—galvanized metal holders that provide firm, secure support.

Finish Components

All other deck parts are considered finish components and are exposed to view. Finish components such as decking, railings, and stairs enhance the appearance and safety of a deck. Components such as railings and stairs are strictly regulated by local building codes, so be sure to check yours before building.

- **Fascia boards** (not illustrated) cover rim joists. They are usually 1-inch-thick boards made from an attractive wood such as cedar or redwood and often cover joists made from pressure-treated lumber. For a clean, finished appearance, fascia may be mitered at the corners. Wood exposed to harsh outdoor climates tends to expand and contract, however, opening even the tightest miter joints over time.
- **Decking** covers joists and forms the main surface area. Decking usually is installed flat and fastened with galvanized nails or screws. Decking boards are spaced ⅛ to 3⁄16 inch apart to provide drainage and allow the wood to contract and expand.

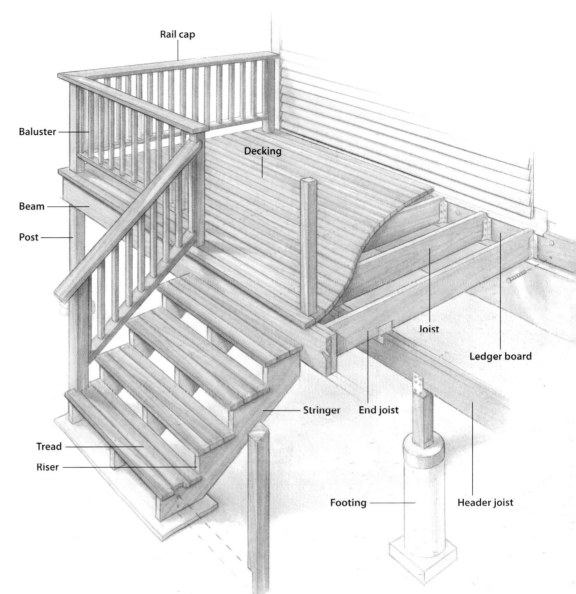

- **Stair and railing systems** are safety features and a major component of deck design. Railing systems comprise posts for support, horizontal rails, and vertical balusters set between the rails. Stairs typically include treads, stringers, and risers. Learn more about railing systems on pages 86–89 and stairs on pages 92–93.
- **Built-ins and overheads** are ancillary structures that provide shade, permit growing plants, create additional seating, and add character to a deck. Learn more about overheads and built-ins on pages 96–99.

DECKING

Decking is the largest visible component of your deck. In its most basic form, decking should provide a durable surface that's free from cracks, splinters, and other defects. Decking also should be attractive and pair with railings and other elements to help set the style of your outdoor living space. Developments in wood alternatives and an increasing number of wood species available for decking enhance your options.

Wood

Natural wood decking features attractive grain patterns. Most wood turns silvery gray when exposed to the elements. If wood color is a factor in your selection, plan to regularly clean and seal it to preserve the original color. Several species are commonly used as decking.

Bamboo—a grass rather than a wood—is a relative newcomer to decking. With its popularity on the rise as an environmentally friendly interior flooring material, bamboo for exterior use is a natural development. Bamboo decking is bonded with a resin to increase its outdoor durability.

Cambara, often referred to as a mahogany, is a hardwood with a reddish-brown color. Though very durable it requires annual application of a finish to keep it looking its best.

Cedar has streaks of cream and brown with occasional knots. It is lightweight and resistant to rot and decay.

Cypress is a soft wood with a varied grain pattern. Lightweight and naturally resistant to rot and decay, cypress is most readily available in the South.

Ipe, a tropical hardwood, boasts a lustrous brown color. Its hardness makes it difficult to cut and drill, but once installed it's impervious to the elements, resists insect damage, and has the same fire rating as concrete or steel.

Jarrah is another hardwood with striking color and grain. Similar to other hardwoods it has the longevity of composite decking.

Mahogany once was commonly used to craft boats because of its resistance to water damage, which makes it suitable as decking. Several subspecies come under the category of mahogany. Cambara is often referred to as mahogany. Meranti—a hardwood with color ranging from light red to a dark reddish brown—is also commonly placed in this category of woods.

Redwood features a distinctive red hue and tight, uniform grain. Naturally resistant to rot and decay, redwood needs to be treated with clear sealers each year to help maintain its color.

Teak, like mahogany, once was commonly used to build ship decks. Because of increasingly depleted supplies, teak is expensive and difficult to find.

Pressure-Treated Wood

Before 2004 pressure-treated lumber was treated with harmful chemicals. Today's versions contain fewer toxins but still resist damage from moisture, decay, and insects. Most pressure-treated woods contain a metal, typically copper. Yet some companies are offering a treated wood product free from metals—it instead uses carbon-base preservatives to protect the wood without the potentially adverse effects of copper. Treated wood typically is green, though brown treated wood is also available. This type of wood can be stained or painted.

Roll-out Decking

Versatile and easy to transport, roll-out decking allows you to extend a current deck, create an instant deck wherever desired, or disguise an unattractive surface beneath decking. Roll-out decking comes in a variety of materials, including cypress and Trex, to enhance your landscape. Another bonus: It's rot- and termite-resistant.

As you'd expect maintenance is minimal for roll-out decking, but as with a built-in deck, it pays to follow these tips to keep your roll-out decking in top form:

Place the deck over a level surface such as sand, gravel, or grass.

Mow the grass underneath at least once a week if you choose a grassy surface.

Clean the deck at least once a year to preserve it.

The rich finish of redwood instantly warms this outdoor kitchen and complements the terra-cotta accents to instill a luxurious look.

Synthetic composite decking boasts an attractive finish and can be easily cleaned with a hose.

Decking laid in a basic pattern gets a style update with alternating boards painted white and gray, *below*. A container of pink flowers adds a colorful counterpoint.

Furniturelike in appearance this durable ipe wood decking serves as an eyecatching complement to the handsome gazebo and wicker seating.

Composite and Synthetic Decking

Advances in synthetic and composite decking have improved the appearance and performance of these products.

Aluminum decking doesn't warp, rot, or crack, and it remains cooler than wood. Some varieties of aluminum decking come with interlocking pieces that prevent water from seeping through the cracks so anything underneath your deck is kept dry.

Composite lumber mixes wood fibers with resins for a deck board that looks similar to wood and has antifungal, light, and moisture protection. Because the boards remain smoother than wood decking, they are

friendly to bare feet. Most composite lumber comes in a variety of natural wood colors. Although the boards have a grain that makes them look more like wood than other synthetic products, the uniform appearance of the grain may be a giveaway that it's not natural.

Plastic decking is environmentally friendly because it is made from recycled material. It typically is available in several natural wood hues as well as in colors designed to look like painted wood. Some plastic decking looks like a woodgrain texture.

Rubber lumber, while not as common as other synthetic options, is an environmentally friendly product that is made from the recycled rubber from old tires and recycled plastics. Though it comes in only a few colors, it's tough and durable.

Vinyl decking offers the same low-maintenance properties as plastic or aluminum decking. The pattern of its nonslip textured surface can be subtly organic, but this type of decking doesn't closely resemble wood. Vinyl decking is available in a variety of colors.

Decking Materials

MATERIAL	PROPERTIES	PRICE
Bamboo	• Environmentally friendly grass • Bonded with resin for outdoor durability	$4.80–$6.50 per square foot
Cedar	• Lightweight • Resistant to rot and decay	$4.00–$7.50 per square foot
Composite	• Wood fibers mixed with resins • Looks similar to wood • Uniform pattern • Low-maintenance; most resist mold, mildew, stains, and fading	$3.00–$7.20 per square foot
Cypress	• Lightweight • Resistant to rot and decay • Most readily available in the South	$2.00–$4.00 per square foot
Exotic hardwoods (cambara, ipe, jarrah, mahogany, teak, and others)	• Hard • Durable • Can be difficult to work with because of hardness • Rich colors ranging from light red to deep brown	$3.00–$7.00 per square foot
Pressure-treated	• Strong • Treated to resist moisture, decay, and insect damage • Typically greenish color but can be stained or painted	$2.00–$4.50 per square foot
Redwood	• Naturally resists rot and decay • Reddish hue that must be sealed annually to maintain	$5.00–$7.00 per square foot
Synthetics (aluminum, plastic, rubber, vinyl)	• Plastic and rubber types are made from environmentally friendly recycled materials	$4.00–$10.00 per square foot

DECKING PATTERNS

Look for opportunities to spice up your deck. The pattern created by decking boards can make a subtle design statement. Typically decking is installed in long rows parallel to the house. Add visual interest by installing decking diagonally or use patterns to break up the expanse of a large deck. Plan your decking design on paper to avoid partial grids or incomplete patterns at the perimeter. Some patterns require extra joists or structural framing for adequate support, so finalize your plans for the decking before construction begins.

Decking patterns can be an important design element. Each pattern, *right*, must have a particular joist layout so that the ends of the decking boards are adequately supported.

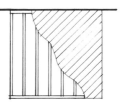

Single diagonal

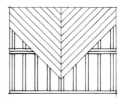

Chevron

Perpendicular

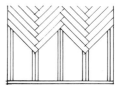

Herringbone

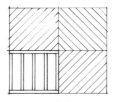

Modular

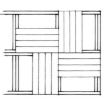

Basket weave

The curved perimeter of this deck provides the opportunity for eye-catching arched boards that follow the angle of the steps.

Invisible fasteners are inexpensive and can help prevent split boards, surface depressions, and popped nails.

Quality fasteners are essential. Coated fasteners made for decks provide the best protection.

FASTENERS

A fastener's main responsibility, of course, is to hold your deck together securely. Beyond that critical function deck fasteners can have a big effect on the look of your deck. When the right fasteners are installed correctly, they'll help prevent decking from splitting, will remain neatly secured to the deck components for years, and won't stain or discolor the decking. Fasteners not suited for the decking materials or those installed improperly can result in protruding fasteners, split boards, and unattractive discoloration.

Structural Fasteners

These fasteners connect the support structure of the deck, so they're typically out of sight once the decking is attached. Heavy-duty screws and bolts are used to fasten large posts and attach the ledger to the house. Framing hardware connects joists to a ledger or beam. A post cap secures a beam to the top of a post, and a post anchor secures a post to a concrete pier.

Decking Fasteners

Nails, screws, and hidden decking connectors are the three main options for attaching decking.

Nails hold fairly well, but some can split wood if holes aren't predrilled. Ringshank and spiral nails grip wood better and are less likely than common nails and box nails to work their way out.

Screws hold better than nails because they have less tendency to pop out of the wood. Look for decking screws coated for resistance to the elements.

Invisible fasteners make your deck more aesthetically pleasing because you won't see them once they're installed. Design advances have made hidden fasteners easier to install. While some still require underdeck installation, which presents problems with low-level decks, many new clips can be installed from above.

Design Tip

Pay close attention when selecting fasteners. New alternatives to pressure-treated wood may have an increased amount of copper and are more likely to react with standard galvanized fasteners. If your decking contains copper, your best bets are stainless-steel and copper fasteners.

RAILINGS

Railings provide a perfect opportunity to add style to a deck. Innovative railing systems in a variety of materials and colors that coordinate with virtually any exterior style have taken deck design to a new level. Choices include copper pipe, galvanized aluminum mesh, aluminum and stainless-steel cables, glass, vinyl, metal, cabling, and composites. Handcrafted railings are another possibility. Before selecting a railing check building codes. Many horizontal rail styles are popular but can pose a safety hazard because young children can climb them like a ladder. If you desire a glass railing that doesn't impede the views, make certain it's constructed from safety glass. Coatings can be applied that create a more scratch- and impact-resistant surface.

No matter the look or material, select a railing style that pairs well with the deck and the house while instilling character. Look for decorative post caps that echo the shape of architectural details—such as trim on an eave or a cornice—on the house. Or choose post caps that house low-voltage outdoor lights. Balusters may be elaborate with flutes, ridges, and grooves. Wood may be left natural, stained, or painted. Try contrasting railing color with house color for a bold statement or use coordinating hues for a more cohesive look.

Design Tip

Decorative post caps top off your deck with style. You'll find caps in a variety of shapes, colors, and materials to suit your taste—the options are endless. Choose caps that complement your deck design or select ones that echo the design of your house to create a more unified look.

The post-and-glass railings that wrap around this redwood deck, which extends 8 feet over a hillside, preserve stunning views without compromising safety.

To create unity the same wood was used to construct this deck, railing, and bench. The railing's rounded post caps add a decorative touch.

A white railing follows the curves of this spacious deck, coordinating with the style of the overhead structure and outdoor furnishings.

Railing Safety

To ensure that your railings are sturdy and secure, consider these pointers:

Test the sturdiness of your railing by moving it back and forth. If it wobbles even a little bit, you need to add support.

Make sure the space between balusters is less than 4 inches so children and pets can't squeeze through. Avoid or use caution with horizontal railings if you have children who can climb the rails.

Use tempered glass if your heart is set on a railing with unobstructed views. To prevent birds from hitting the glass, select a slightly tinted variety.

Follow the same building codes for built-in benches along the edge of the deck as you would for railings. Make sure the bench is 36 to 42 inches high if the deck is more than 24 inches above ground.

This railing provides necessary security for a raised deck while the basic white hue and straightforward styling keep attention focused on the lake beyond.

This detailed copper cap, shaped by a router, provides a striking contrast to a classic white railing.

DESIGN GALLERY
Railings

The main purpose of a railing is to provide safety and support—but why not have a little fun with it? A well-designed railing adds personality, so consider giving your deck a decorative touch with these ideas.

1

1: A post cap adds an appropriate finishing touch to this railing. Post caps are available in a variety of materials and designs to coordinate with railing, deck, and house styles.

2: Painted in different colors, triangle-shape blocks add a whimsical touch to this wood deck. The railing is hollow in the middle to echo the style of the slatted wood steps.

3: A sharp black and white color scheme defines this railing, which features shapely curvilinear balusters.

4: Sturdy stainless-steel cables create a cool counterpoint against a colorful railing and provide unobstructed views from the deck.

5: A decorative railing doesn't have to be elaborate to stand out. These evenly spaced diamond-shape accents add subtle flair to an otherwise plain deck.

2

A vertical wrought-iron railing coordinates with the furnishings on this deck. The simple railing design accommodates open views.

STAIRS & RAMPS

Stairs offer an easy transition from the interior of your house to the deck and yard. Position the stairs to take advantage of natural traffic patterns rather than forcing people to walk around seating areas, dining space, or an outdoor kitchen. Stairs should be wide enough for two people to pass comfortably. Building codes govern the specifics of stair construction, but there is room for creativity within the guidelines.

Low platform decks might not require railings and instead can feature wide stairs that span the perimeter, creating an ideal, expansive transition to the yard. A particularly high raised deck might benefit from a landing platform midway down the run of stairs. If space allows the platform might contain a built-in bench or planter for a decorative touch. Also consider including one or two turns in a long run of stairs so the stairs don't project awkwardly into the yard.

Ramps make accessing the deck easy for everyone. Ramp slope should be gentle and follow building code guidelines for suitable rise and run. Make certain the ramp is wide enough to allow someone in a wheelchair ample room to navigate. As with a long stairway, if the ramp will be long, plan for a series of turns with spacious landings. Include a concrete pad at the bottom for traction. And, as with stairs, use materials and colors for the ramp that integrate with the rest of the deck and the house.

These wide platform steps connect harmoniously with the rest of the shallow deck. Potted plants and a pergola help ease the transition.

Wide, sloping ramps are ideal for wheelchair accessibility, *right*. The board placement also helps: These are perpendicular on slopes and diagonal on landings to improve traction.

The recessed design of this staircase, *below*, eliminates the need for a railing. Instead strategically placed lighting enhances nighttime walking safety.

The Craftsman-style mahogany staircase complements the home's architecture. Wood plugs hide the screws that attach the planks.

White lattice skirting complements the deck and house instead of competing with them.

SKIRTING & SCREENS

Skirting

Skirting plays a decorative and functional role. It hides the structural components of a deck and, depending on its construction, can minimize the opportunity for animals and debris to gather under the deck. The best skirting has small openings to allow air to circulate while keeping out all but the tiniest of creatures. Prefabricated skirting is readily available but can visually compete with other deck elements such as railings and stairs. Paint or stain skirting a natural color—such as brown or gray—to camouflage it. The most attractive types of skirting typically are custom-made to coordinate with the deck style, materials, and color. If possible install skirting in pieces that can be removed for underdeck maintenance. Or install one section on a hinge so that it can be opened easily. Planning foundation plantings around the base of a deck can help conceal part of the skirting. Skirting is not a requirement, however. In fact the structural components of many decks make striking architectural statements that are best left visible.

Screens

While skirting conceals what's under your deck, screens help shelter what's on it. Screen out an unwanted view of garbage cans next door. Or obstruct views of your deck from a nosy neighbor's backyard. A screen can function as a wall for the deck, creating a sense of enclosure and fostering intimacy in an otherwise open area. Screens are useful, too, for shading the deck from low, late afternoon rays. As with skirting preassembled lattice screens are readily available. Or for a more dramatic style statement, construct your own screen. For added style integrate a screen with an overhead structure or built-in seating or planters. Train climbing vines such as clematis and trumpet vines to grow on the screen for added privacy and a lush look complete with gorgeous blooms.

This skirting, *right*, retains its natural finish and maintains the rustic look of the deck above. Because it's placed low to the ground, wood skirting should be made from rot-resistant wood.

Crafted from the same old-growth western red cedar as the deck, this screen enhanced by climbing vines, *above*, provides privacy from the house next door.

OVERHEAD STRUCTURES

Overheads can help transform your deck into an outdoor living room by creating shade, establishing a welcome sense of enclosure, and adding character and style. The classic look of a post-and-beam pergola with a wealth of architectural details is a suitable partner for a Colonial house. Repeating design motifs found on the house is another option. For example a pergola with river-rock bases and painted post caps might echo the design of a Craftsman-style house.

Whatever the style you'll want your pergola to last so choose durable rot-resistant materials. These structures usually are custom made, but prepackaged kits are also available. Overheads can be freestanding or extend from the house. In either case at least a couple of posts must be anchored into the ground with concrete footings or securely fastened to the deck. Reinforce beams that will support the heaviest loads by adding braces.

The amount of shade and protection an overhead provides depends on the spacing of its slats. To effectively cut the sun's rays, place the lattice or other slats close together. For a more weather-resistant outdoor space, consider a solid-roof structure instead.

Design Tip

Define your outdoor room with a ceiling, walls, and a floor. The decking is the floor, while your home's exterior or a vine-covered lattice screen might serve as the walls. A full roof will protect you from sun and rain, while overhead structures such as a pergola create shelter without complete enclosure.

Shaded by surrounding Douglas fir trees, this pergola designates an intimate space for dining while still letting in filtered sun.

This stately pergola is proportionate to the house and yard. The varied spacing of the rafters allows for a pleasing mix of sun and shade.

Built-in seating can be freestanding, like this Y-shape bench. Attractive flower containers placed in each corner distinguish the slatted-wood seat from the rest of the deck.

BUILT-INS

Built-ins help personalize and add comfort and convenience to a deck. Benches, planters, storage components, and outdoor cooking areas are all possible built-in elements. (See pages 156–159 for more about outdoor kitchens.)

Beyond providing permanent seating, built-in benches offer the same type of cozy relaxation spot as an indoor window seat. Look for opportunities to create built-in benches with backrests for the most comfortable seating. Built-in benches along the perimeter of the deck may substitute for a standard railing, depending on the height of your deck and local building code requirements.

Built-in planters bring the beauty of flowering plants and greenery onto the deck. On low-platform decks they can help define the edges of the structure. On other decks planters can be integrated with the railing or positioned at the ends of a bench. Planters should be made from a moisture-resistant material and have drainage holes at the bottom that extend through the decking. This will help prevent rotting or other moisture-related damage. To keep the sides of a planter looking good, line it with a waterproof membrane.

Storage compartments are a handy built-in option. Benches with hinged tops might disguise waterproof containers ideal for stowing outdoor toys, cushions, and blankets right where they are needed.

This curved built-in bench blends with the rest of the multilevel deck and offers a stunning view of the landscape beyond.

An abundance of large and small shrubs fill these tiered built-in planters. The layered look of the planters and shrubs adds dimension.

A built-in bench doubles as the railing for this low deck. Check with a building inspector to see whether a built-in bench can be used in place of a railing.

A coat of white paint gives this deck an airy look. To keep a painted deck looking good, you may have to scrape, sand, and repaint it periodically.

FINISHING & MAINTENANCE

Though certainly not as enjoyable as relaxing on your deck, selecting the right finish and protecting it with simple, ongoing maintenance is the best way to ensure that you'll be able to take advantage of your outdoor space for years.

Wood decks benefit from the application of a finish that minimizes drying, cracking, and fading.

Clear finishes seal the wood against moisture loss and help prolong its natural beauty. To best protect the natural color of the wood and minimize graying, select a finish with UV blockers. Even then to best maintain original beauty the decking should be thoroughly cleaned and refinished each year.

Stains alter the appearance of the decking and are ideal for pressure-treated wood that commonly has a greenish cast. Stains vary from semitransparent, which allows the grain to show through, to solid that hides grain patterns. Solid stains are ideal if you want a uniform look free from the natural flaws found in most wood. Test the stain on scrap decking before application to make sure you like the look.

Paint is another finish option though it's not usually recommended because exposure to the elements and foot traffic can cause it to crack, peel, and fade. Maintaining a painted deck requires periodic scraping, sanding, and repainting. If you want to add color to a deck, consider painting the railing or an overhead structure or selecting a color stain instead.

Design Tip

When exposed to weather conditions from blazing sun to heavy rains or snow, rich wood surfaces such as cedar and redwood tend to develop an unsightly silvery gray finish. Preserve your wood's natural color by cleaning the surface and applying a clear sealer every year.

Proper maintenance helps to
maintain the wood's uniform
appearance.

DESIGN GALLERY
Deck Trends

A true classic never goes out of style—it just needs an occasional update, as these deck trends prove. By giving traditional features a modern update, you can infuse your deck with timeless style and function.

1: More than the typical pergola, this frame benefits from beautiful architectural details and a rich green hue.

2: Built-in flowerboxes take the concept of raised beds to a new level and serve as a natural boundary on this deck. The plantings create bursts of color.

3: The clean, straight lines of this open deck are a nod to modern minimalist design. The deck was built around the existing landscape so it blends with the striking scenery.

4: Shaded by a narrow arbor, this sunny deck boasts handy built-in seating to supplement the freestanding furnishings nearby.

5: A curvy deck offers a fresh alternative to sharp-edge versions. Distinctive detailing on the pergola adds architectural interest.

1: Woodlike in appearance this deck is made from fade-resistant synthetic decking. Echoing the home's architecture, the structure looks like a natural extension instead of an afterthought.

2: This two-story deck takes outdoor living to the next-level—literally—with several distinct zones for relaxation. The unique green, red, and white color palette makes the structure stand out.

3: A cool gray hue and lush foliage integrated into the design make this simple multilevel deck pop with personality.

4: Stately white features give this deck Colonial charm. The ipe floor contrasts with the creamy white hue.

5: This multilevel deck is abloom with fiberglass planters that ease the transition from deck to landscape. The deck's graceful curves resemble a cascading waterfall.

CHAPTER 5

Patio Basics

*Patio Styles, Patio Construction, Materials, Brick, Concrete,
Stone, Tile, Loose Materials & Combinations,
Shade & Privacy, Accents, Finishing & Maintenance*

Do you envision a spacious patio for large gatherings or a cozy area for intimate conversation? Either way pulling your desired look together is easier than you think. As you read this chapter, you'll see a variety of patio styles to suit your property. Gather basic tips for constructing your patio. From formal-looking brick to a casual sprinkling of loose gravel, the right surface material is essential in establishing the function and mood of the space. You'll find the pros and cons of each material in this chapter. In addition learn to transform your patio into a custom masterpiece with well-placed accents. Tips for keeping your patio in great shape are here too because a well-maintained patio is your ticket to comfortably enjoying the outdoors.

Creating a large, flat concrete patio may require grading the backyard. To avoid that expense consider working with the terrain instead. With its flagstone surface this patio looks natural even in areas that aren't flat. Contoured edging was designed to flow around trees and shrubs rather than forcing their removal.

A small patio extends this home's outdoor living space beyond the screen porch. A short brick retaining wall defines the edges of the concrete patio.

PATIO STYLES

The size and style of a patio depend on how you plan to use it. It should be a comfortable, well-planned solution to your family's needs. If you expect to use your patio only for occasional family barbecues or for relaxing and reading, a small patio may be sufficient. If you entertain often perhaps the solution is an area large enough for guests to comfortably converse, mingle, and dine. A well-designed patio can feature different areas that fulfill a variety of purposes. This may include cooking centers, meditative retreats, and more. Listing your primary goals is the first step toward determining the patio style that best fits your lifestyle.

A patio is placed directly on the ground, and the final design often depends on the shape of the terrain. To some extent the land can be altered into a new topography. If extensive site work is in the plans, your checkbook may take a hit. Such work can cost thousands of dollars if it involves grading your land and adding retaining walls.

Before you call in the bulldozers to carve out the backyard you think you want, consider other options that could be more cost effective. Imaginative design often solves problems, including uneven land or steep grades. For instance creating a series of smaller, stepped patios is one solution.

Design Tip

Even a small backyard can be the perfect spot for creating an outdoor escape. To make a small patio seem cozy and secluded rather than cramped, simplicity rules. Increase the usable area on the patio by placing carefully selected furnishings along the sides so the center remains open. Another idea: Trick the eye into thinking the patio is larger than it is by drawing attention to the space around the patio. Blurring patio borders with plantings can lead the eye outward.

The drain on the floor of this patio, *above*, channels moisture away to prevent standing water in the event of heavy rain or a fountain overflow.

A small rooftop patio relies on raised planters to create distinct zones for lounging and sitting, *left*.

Design Tip

Screen patios allow you to enjoy your outdoor space longer. Made of fiberglass mesh, stainless steel, or regular window screening, screen patios keep pesky insects at bay. Use glass to transform your patio into a sunroom with four-season appeal. Add privacy with shades or awnings.

Built into the patio a gazebo serves as an enclosed retreat that allows spacious views and offers protection from weather extremes.

Careful attention to detail ensures a level surface and a good fit between paving materials on this patio.

PATIO CONSTRUCTION

Patio construction is relatively simple but physically demanding. Patios are built in layers. Soil must be removed to create a level base. A bottom layer typically compacted gravel—is spread and leveled to create a solid foundation for the paving materials. To minimize weed growth between the paving materials, consider placing a sheet of landscape fabric on top of the base. Next a thin sand base is spread and leveled. Then the pavers of your choosing are set into the sand. Finally, grout is applied. For dry-fit applications, sand or dry mortar mix is spread between the pavers to help hold them in place. For a more stable foundation, a concrete slab may be poured over the gravel subbase. Paving materials are set on the patio base and grouted with mortar mix to inhibit movement.

Groundcover between pavers provides essential definition for this checkerboard-inspired design.

Patios needn't always be constructed flat on the ground. This one emulates a raised deck, complete with stairs leading to the yard beyond.

MATERIALS

Patios have made a significant backyard comeback—and it's no wonder with the plethora of gorgeous paving materials available to bring texture, color, and pattern to your outdoor living space. Go ahead: Mix and match paving materials to weave your own landscape tapestry. Just avoid introducing too many materials or you'll have a hodgepodge rather than a pleasing design. Think of your patio as an outdoor room that links the house to the surrounding landscape. You even can extend paving material vertically to create walls, fireplaces, and an outdoor kitchen area. If you have a large expanse to cover, vary materials to distinguish one outdoor room from another. To make a small outdoor area look larger, use the same color and type of material throughout.

With its unified pattern, this brick patio surface sets the stage for a formal garden and adds timeless character throughout the space. A wrought-iron bistro table topped with a lacy white tablecloth and bouquet-filled urn adds to the classic style.

The distinct rectangular shape of brick provides a pleasing contrast to the kidney-shape swimming pool. The pattern of the bricks adds further variety.

BRICK

Brick remains a popular, moderately priced option for patios. Reddish-hue bricks lend a classic look to almost any setting. Or choose from a range of colors to coordinate with your house and any existing hardscapes. Brick can be mortared in cement for a finished look, but the mortar may deteriorate in time. Dry-fitting bricks are another option.

Types
New brick comes in several grades, including severe weather grade bricks that are designed to withstand temperature extremes and moisture conditions that can cause chipping or breaking in less sturdy grades. Less porous than other types, severe-weather bricks also are more resistant to staining. Paving bricks are designed to withstand the extreme conditions faced by a patio. They're particularly hard and resistant to moisture and therefore an excellent choice for patios. If you prefer a touch of old-world charm, consider used brick. Typically salvaged from old buildings, used brick has a worn, rustic character. Because these bricks are old, they might not be as hard and durable as new ones. And used brick might not be consistent in size and shape, so plan the pattern carefully.

Patterns

Bricks' modular shape lends well to creative patterns that boost style. Varying the pattern on a large patio is a good way to distinguish functional areas. Even complex styles are fairly easy to install with some planning. Keep in mind that the more complex the pattern and the more curves in the overall design, the more bricks you'll have to cut—a time-intensive activity that will increase the cost of your patio.

Brick patterns can be an important design element. Each pattern, *right*, must be planned in advance. The more complex the design, the longer the installation will take.

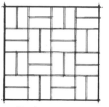

Basket weave

Jack on Jack

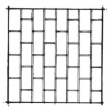

Running bond

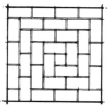

Spiral

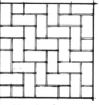

Herringbone

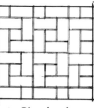

Pinwheel

The reddish hue of the bricks that line this patio exudes warmth. A smaller swath of brick below the stairs eases the transition to the lawn.

The formed brick surface of this patio, which is broken up by expanses of trees and plantings, exudes a sense of rustic style.

CONCRETE

Forget the dreary slab patios of the past. Concrete has come into its own with a bevy of options that give it a whole new twist. If your outdoor room is stuck in a time warp with an old but intact concrete patio, consider acid etching. This process scores and roughens an existing slab to give it a new look similar to stone. Tired of that dull gray slab? Chemical stains can be applied to nearly obliterate the drab color and imbue the space with hues ranging from pastels to deep organic colors. For a new concrete patio, the options are even more varied. Concrete is versatile and can easily be formed into a variety of sizes and shapes including curves. A drawback of concrete is its tendency to crack. Control joints—narrow

Staying true to its natural hue, this concrete patio lets a bright white raised planter bursting with pink blossoms stand out as its dominant feature.

A gray patio surface provides a cool counterpoint to a warm red brick border. The concrete's light hue makes the patio appear more spacious.

A stamped-concrete patio designed to
look like stone pavers lends definition and
functionality to a narrow property.

Doing double duty as a pool surround and a patio, this concrete surface boasts a light hue that is more likely to stay cool beneath bare feet.

seams in the patio—will reduce the likelihood of cracking and should be planned to integrate with the overall design.

Surface Finishes

A textured concrete surface is more visually appealing and less slippery than a perfectly smooth one. Small stones can be sprinkled over the concrete while it's wet to create a rustic, pebbly finish that is especially good near pools and other wet areas. Broom-finish surfaces have a subtle pattern created when a stiff broom is brushed on a damp concrete surface. The resulting tiny ridges increase traction. Wet concrete also may be stamped with plastic molds for patterns that resemble brick, tile, stone, or leaf imprints.

Color

Color options are greater for new concrete patios than for existing ones. Adding color to concrete is not like applying paint to a wall, however; the resulting color will depend on the composition of the concrete, the timing of the application, and the temperature when it's poured. While you do choose the desired color, be prepared for the actual results to vary.

A little color goes a long way when punching up a concrete patio. Embedded in concrete, ceramic tiles arranged in a loose floral pattern give this patio a major style update.

Color pigment that is added to premixed concrete before it is poured extends through the entire slab and minimizes the appearance of cracks and chips that develop over time. Finished colors are more muted with this technique than with dust-on or chemical staining. Dust-on color is applied to the wet surface of a newly poured slab. Because the color is concentrated in the top layer of concrete, the finished color is more vibrant than that of the color pigment. Chemical staining or color etching requires cured concrete. To apply this technique to a new patio, the concrete must cure for a month or more.

PAVERS

Concrete pavers come in a variety of shapes, sizes, colors, and textures. Made from cast concrete, pavers are a tough, durable material ideal for patio surfaces. Their modular shape allows for the creation of all the patterns you can form with bricks and more. Paver shapes include circles, diamonds, hexagons, octagons, and crescents. To ease the pattern-forming process, look for pavers that have beveled sides for circular patterns or interlocking designs that fit together like a puzzle. Color possibilities include a range of muted earth tones—consider a design that features several colors to enhance the pattern. Some pavers have a thin pigment layer that allows gray to show when they're scratched or chipped, so look for pavers with a thick color layer.

Concrete pavers can work well combined with other patio materials. Tumbled concrete pavers team with Buckingham slate to create an engaging foursquare pattern, *above*.

Living grout—in the form of Elfin thyme and Turkish Veronica—gives these pavers a bountiful look that ties in with the landscape, *left*.

A simple layout of subtle pavers allows other elements on a patio—such as this beautiful fence and a fountain and pond surrounded by boulders—to steal the show.

Timeless Pennsylvania bluestone sets the stage for an alfresco entertaining spot.

STONE

The enduring quality and distinct beauty of natural stone make it hard to beat as an outdoor paving material. Stone comes in many colors and textures, enabling it to work well with a variety of architectural styles. Although it is usually the most expensive paving option, stone adds permanent value and beauty.

To select the best stone for your patio, consider qualities, colors, and availability. Stone varies in hardness and porosity. Patios made from a hard stone will last much longer than those of soft stone. Porous stones will absorb water and are more prone to cracking when the water freezes and expands. Regional stone will be more readily available in your area and will cost less than stone that must be shipped long distances to your site.

Flagstone

Most patio stone is flagstone, a term that refers to the shape of the stone rather than its type. Flagstone describes stone cut into slabs ideal for paving. Split-face flagstone presents a rough, uneven surface, while

Loose-cut stone interspersed in a concrete bed creates an attractive pool walkway that's low-maintenance so attention can be focused on having fun in the sun.

honed flagstone has been smoothed by a machine for a more even face. Consider how you will use the patio and the look you want when choosing between split-face and honed stones. Outdoor dining areas may benefit from a honed finish so chairs and tables are less prone to wobbling. Likewise if young children regularly play on the patio, they'll have steadier footing on a honed surface. The most common choices for flagstone are limestone, sandstone, slate, granite, and bluestone. Each has a range of colors so examine samples of the stone to find the color that best complements your design.

Flagstone pieces typically range from quite small to 2 feet across. Installers will prefit the pieces much like a puzzle to accomplish the best layout for your patio.

Stone Tiles

If you like the look of natural stone but want a more even surface than flagstone presents, consider stone tiles. Many types of stone—including marble, slate, sandstone, limestone, and granite—can be cut into tiles. The labor of shaping the stone will drive up the cost. Stone tiles must be set on a foundation of poured concrete with grout between the tiles to hold them in place.

River Rocks

Rocks that have been worn smooth by water are durable, moisture-resistant, and inexpensive. Their rounded shape, however, limits their usefulness for patio applications. Large pieces can be used as decorative accents along the perimeter of a patio or walkway. Very small river rocks can be used for loose installations or set in concrete. (See pages 130–131 for more information.)

Stone tiles with a well-worn patina complement a rough flagstone border.

This courtyard dining area is distinguished by a loose gravel floor. Small, tightly packed gravel is easier for walking and sitting.

Quadrants of timeworn brick mingle effortlessly with flagstone to create a casual outdoor dining area filled with warm, natural red hues.

TILE

If you want a polished outdoor space that looks like an extension of the interior, tile provides the ultimate finished look. Installed on a concrete slab, tile must be rated for outdoor flooring use so it is durable, moisture-resistant, and low-maintenance. For the best results select a nonporous, slip-resistant tile. Porous tiles will absorb water—in cold climates this could cause them to freeze and expand, resulting in cracked tile. Tiles are available glazed and unglazed, but unglazed or matte-finish ones will be less slippery.

Ceramic tile offers the widest range of colors because a ceramic coating is bonded to the clay body during firing. Glazing helps tiles resist stains and moisture. Check the hardness rating to make sure a glazed ceramic tile is suitable for flooring.

Porcelain tiles are extremely hard and stain-resistant. Look for slip-resistant textures ideal for outdoor use. Though almost all tiles require grouting to set them, interlocking porcelain tiles are available. Just click the tiles into position over a hard, level, and smooth surface.

Quarry tile is a mixture of clay and shale. Typically unglazed quarry tile is available in a variety of natural earth tones including dark reds, yellows, grays, and browns. Its slightly textured finish makes it an ideal slip-resistant outdoor material.

Terra-cotta tiles are common in Southwestern outdoor spaces. Originally handmade tiles noted for their natural variations and imperfections, terra-cotta tiles now include processed styles with clean edges and smooth surfaces. Typically unglazed, these tiles have natural clay colors including ocher and umber. Most are at least somewhat porous so check for installation recommendations in your region.

Brightened by cool cobalt blue accents, this saltillo tile floor coordinates with stucco walls and blue accents for a unified look.

The straight edges of this bluestone tile patio complement the formality of the pavilion. The varied grout lines provide traction.

Scattered rocks underfoot create a casual look and provide sufficient drainage opportunities for the abundant plant life in this space.

Loose materials are a natural fit for this patio, which also contains a pergola and bench made from twigs and sticks.

LOOSE MATERIALS & COMBINATIONS

The crunch of gravel underfoot along a path or on an informal patio adds to the casual ambience of outdoor living. From a practical standpoint loose materials including gravel and river rock provide good drainage. Aesthetically they offer interesting textures for patio surfaces. The same qualities that make loose materials pleasing also can present drawbacks. Loose materials tend to spread over time and therefore require containment within a border such as larger stone, brick, or wood. To prevent weed growth position a layer of landscape fabric before spreading loose paving. Consider how you will use the space before selecting a material. Gravel, crushed rock, and lava rock have sharp edges that are uncomfortable for bare feet while river rock is naturally smooth and rounded. Gravel packs well to form a stable base; river rock remains loose and does not pack well. Some applications may be unsuitable for any type of loose material. A frequently used outdoor dining space, for example, may benefit from a more solid foundation that acts as a sturdy base for a table and chairs.

Combining Materials

As outdoor living increases in popularity, patios have become larger and more elaborate. Many of these spaces

Design Tip

Soften the space between your irregularly shaped flagstone pavers with lush green groundcover. This living grout adds character and boasts staying power: It can withstand foot traffic and doesn't wash away. Try flowering thyme, Scotch moss, sedum, candytuft, and alyssum. When installing groundcover make sure flagstones are 2 to 3 inches apart and fill the gaps with high-quality soil.

A pattern of pavers surrounded by flagstones and pebbles gives this patio a distinct, defined look. Another benefit: The contrasting colors and textures make it easy for users to watch where they're stepping.

comprise a series of small patios or are one large patio segmented into various areas according to use. In any of these cases, combining patio materials creates interesting textures and designs and—like floor surface changes indoors—helps distinguish one outdoor room from another. Combining materials works best when they share the same base and are similar in thickness. Otherwise the finished surface will be uneven.

Patio Materials

MATERIAL	PROPERTIES	COST
Brick	• May be dry-fit over gravel and sand base or mortared over concrete • Range of organic colors including tans, grays, reds, and browns • Durable	$1.50–$5.00 per square foot
Ceramic Tile	• Almost unlimited color options • Glossy, glazed tiles can be slippery • Excellent durability with outdoor-rated tiles • Mortared over concrete installation	$5.00–$15.00 per square foot
Concrete	• Excellent durability • Untreated color is dull gray but can be colored • Can be formed into a variety of shapes • May crack • Surface finishes may be applied to give texture	$1.00–$15.00 per square foot
Flagstone	• Many varieties available • Regional varieties will be more readily available and typically less expensive than other varieties • Durability ranges from good to excellent depending on the specific stone • Colors include creams, yellows, grays, reds, browns, dark blues, and variations • May be dry-fit over gravel and sand base or mortared over concrete	$5.00–$11.00 per square foot
Paver	• Excellent durability • Range of shapes and sizes allows for the creation of interesting patterns • Range of organic colors including tans, grays, reds, and browns • May be dry-fit over gravel and sand base or mortared over concrete	$3.00–$8.00 per square foot
River Rock	• Smooth, rounded surface • Difficult to make level surface because of shape • Good for borders and vertical features	$29.00–$55.00 per cubic yard
Stone Tile	• Many varieties available • Durability depends on the particular type of stone • Stone cut into tiles is more even than flagstone	$4.00–$20.00 per square foot
Porcelain Tile	• Extremely hard and stain-resistant • Mortared over concrete installation • Excellent durability	$2.00–$4.00 per square foot
Terra-Cotta Tile	• Many tiles are handmade with unique markings and imperfections • Not as durable as other tiles • Natural clay colors including umber and ocher	$2.00–$7.00 per square foot

DESIGN GALLERY
Patio Materials

The paving materials you choose set the stage for the rest of the design. So why not select something that you'll enjoy for a long time? Put your imagination to good use and try these engaging options.

1

2

1: This curved, stacked brick patio border establishes a formal setting and provides texture against the smooth concrete floor.

2: Artfully arranged and set in concrete, this medley of colored stones creates an attractive design.

3: A bluish-gray honed slate patio contrasts with its red brick border. The irregular shapes of the slate add visual interest.

4: The floor of this patio boasts a foursquare pattern that incorporates slate with tumbled concrete pavers. A river rock base topped with handhewn basalt supports the pergola and fountain.

5: Creative details amplify small spaces. Here a figure-eight design is tucked into a small patio area. The wood border and chairs add texture.

This gazebo's windows were strategically positioned to overlook the surrounding scenery, a design that allows great views without sacrificing privacy.

SHADE & PRIVACY

Shade

Filtered shade helps create an ideal outdoor living space. Too much shade and you might as well be indoors; too little shade during the hottest part of the day and you'll seek relief elsewhere. If you're fortunate enough to have a yard with large, mature, deciduous trees, try to position the patio where it benefits from generous shade in the summer. In the spring when the leaves are beginning to grow and in the autumn when the leaves fall, more sunlight will reach the patio.

If your yard is lacking mature trees, an overhead structure is a good solution for instant sun protection. Position the slats close together for more shade or spread them apart for lighter shade. Overheads may include side screens or slats to provide relief from the low rays of late afternoon sun.

Privacy

Your patio should feel like a private retreat. While the ideal level of privacy for your patio depends on its use, plan for at least some privacy so your patio won't serve

A grand pergola encloses the dining area of this otherwise wide-open rooftop garden, making it an enjoyable setting for dining even on sunny days.

Lattice strips attached to peaked rafters create overhead privacy and provide this sheltered space with dappled sunlight and fresh breezes. Surrounding trees ensure shade on sunny days.

Gazebos

Distinguished by their elegant form and peaked roofs, gazebos create focal point to your outdoor setting. Design your dream gazebo with these tips in mind:

Make sure the architectural style of the gazebo echoes that of your home, especially if the two structures are close. If you have a brick house, try securing your gazebo to a brick base or incorporating bricks in the landscaping around the gazebo.

Let the gazebo blend naturally with its surroundings. For example a shake-shingle roof atop a weathered wood gazebo will enhance cottage-style character.

Have fun when selecting materials. Because gazebos are smaller than homes, you can splurge on more expensive materials such as cedar shakes.

Because this area is in full sun, a garden room was built to provide shade.

as a stage for the neighbors' viewing. Privacy screens block views and provide a sense of enclosure without making you feel walled in. Screens typically are open lattice or slats spaced slightly to allow breezes through. Consider a trellis that supports climbing vines that bloom.

The trellis will provide some privacy during winter and early spring, and by summer it will fill in when the vines leaf out and are blooming. If the screen will be along the perimeter of your property, check building codes that may apply.

This screened wood fence receives additional privacy from flowering trailing vines that blossom with color.

ACCENTS

Turn your patio into a true outdoor room with accents that are beautiful and functional. Structures such as privacy screens and benches make your patio more livable. Turn to Chapter Six (page 144) for more information about amenities such as fireplaces, outdoor kitchens, and pools and spas. Decorative accents personalize the space and make it inviting.

Cedar planters bursting with layered plants provide a vibrant border for this small rooftop patio without taking much space. The planters are tall enough to conceal the railing without obstructing views.

Benches
Many decks have built-in benches, so why not adapt the concept for your patio? A stone wall along the perimeter of the patio can double as seating during a large gathering. Extra-wide steps that lead from a terraced patio to the yard also work as a perch for guests.

A stone-carved lion splashes water into this large built-in fountain designed to help mask noise. Leafy green plants provide a cool contrast to the warm stone.

Water
Splashing fountains and gurgling water features are attractive and provide soothing background noise. Install a wall fountain in a small patio area to enjoy the charm of bubbling water without the space required for a freestanding model. On a large patio consider positioning a round fountain in the center as a dramatic focal point.

Planters

Raised-bed planters lend vertical height and elevate plants to a level where they are easy to water and tend. Planters filled with blooms bring a dash of color to the patio. Building planters from the same material as the patio surface lends continuity. Or select a contrasting material for stronger definition of the perimeter of the space.

Art

A wide array of artful accents is available for outdoor use. Stone urns, metal sculptures, ceramic pots, and glass globes are good options for adding style that can withstand the elements. Apply common decorating principles: Determine a look you like and select objects that extend that style throughout the space. Group smaller objects for impact. Balancing objects throughout the outdoor room helps create a cohesive design theme.

A large white trellis marks the entrance to this patio. Enhanced by ornate detailing that matches the home's trim, the trellis makes a strong decorative and architectural statement.

A light-color patio surface requires occasional sweeping to keep dirt at bay and retain its natural hue.

FINISHING & MAINTENANCE

A little upkeep typically is all that's required to maintain your patio's beauty. Bricks, concrete, and pavers usually require the least care. Their surfaces generally aren't adversely affected by moisture and temperature changes. Just be sure to wipe up spills immediately to reduce the chance of staining and sweep your patio occasionally to remove dirt.

Other patio surface materials may benefit from application of a sealer. Sealers help prevent staining and cracking and chipping from water absorption. Two basic types of sealers are available: surface and penetrating. Surface sealers resist moisture and stains well, but most must be stripped and reapplied every two to three years. Penetrating sealers don't withstand moisture and stains quite as well as surface sealers, but they provide a softer sheen and allow the patio to develop a patina over time. Penetrating sealers can be maintained by simply applying a fresh coat. Check with your paving material provider for recommendations for the right care and maintenance.

If your pavers are surrounded by plants that require regular watering, it's best to apply a sealant that will deter moisture absorption.

Removing Efflorescence

Though it won't damage your patio, efflorescence—a naturally occurring chalky white masonry surface haze—adds an unattractive finish to brick, concrete, concrete pavers, and some stones. Get rid of efflorescence with these tips:

Lightly scrub the surface with a stiff wire brush and soap and water. If you have a brick patio, don't scrub too hard or you might scratch the surface.

Make a weak solution with 1 part muriatic acid (found at masonry supply stores) to 20 parts water and scrub with a brush if plain water doesn't cut it. Be sure to rinse well with water afterward.

Look for commercially prepared solutions at masonry supply stores for removing efflorescence.

DESIGN GALLERY
Patio Trends

Put your patio on the cutting edge with these surefire suggestions for transforming your outdoor areas from dated to dramatic. These trends effectively blend utility and elegance for ultimate staying power.

1: Defined by a zigzag-shape stone border, flowerbeds break up this patio walkway in a way that still allows easy access.

2: Sprinkled between pavers glimmering blue glass elicits the soothing illusion of flowing water. The sharp square shapes of the pavers and pond create a sense of order.

3: Large brick pillars dramatically announce the transition from pool to patio. The classic white hue unites the space to achieve a cottage-fresh look.

4: Filled with low-maintenance succulents, these colorful vintage planters play off the hues of the landscape. Look for similar pots at flea markets and antiques stores.

5: Artfully concealed in a wood arbor, a copper gutter recycles rainwater to create a cascading fountain that offers smooth sounds and aids irrigation.

1: Small accents can make a small patio come alive with personality without overwhelming it. Tea lights and pillar candles add an inviting glow to this intimate brick patio.

2: Covered by a tree- and vine-shaded pergola, a walkway that is perfect for an after-dinner stroll connects a garden with the dining patio.

3: Built to look like an extension of the home, this pergola provides perfect shade for the seating area. Natural materials—wood, stone, and plants—infuse the space with rich texture.

4: A rustic stone patio allows enough room for this intimate seating arrangement that takes advantage of serene views.

CHAPTER 6

Amenities

Plumbing, Electricity, Lighting, Fireplaces,
Outdoor Kitchens, Spas & Pools, Paths & Walkways

Outdoor rooms have evolved into functional spaces ideal for entertaining or relaxing thanks to the indoor-inspired amenities you'll see in this chapter. But to take indoor comforts outside, you first need the plumbing and electricity to support them. Ample lighting is a must because it ensures safety and adds ambience. The warmth and soft glow provided by outdoor fireplaces prolong the life of your gatherings. Do you enjoy outdoor dining? An outdoor kitchen may be a solid investment once you determine the setup that suits your culinary needs. Create splashy style with a pool or spa (or both), and visually connect your yard's distinctive spaces with paths and walkways made from any number of interesting materials.

PLUMBING

As outdoor rooms trend toward more elaborate spaces that feature many of the fixtures and amenities found indoors, consider having plumbing run to service your new patio or deck. If the space will include an outdoor kitchen (see pages 156–161 for more about kitchens), plumbing provides the convenience of on-site food preparation and cleanup. If your outdoor haven will have a water feature, outdoor plumbing can simplify the task of refilling it. When your deck or patio serves as a spot from which to appreciate lush gardens, ample water spouts ease the need to snake hoses through the space. Look for a self-draining, freezeproof outdoor faucet; that way if you forget to shut off and drain the line before winter, you shouldn't have any problems. Outdoor showers are increasingly popular as a poolside convenience. An outdoor shower should provide a sense of privacy so look for a tucked-away nook that's close enough to the pool or spa yet out of the main traffic flow.

Weather-resistant cedar or pressure-treated wood that is stained is best for an outdoor shower structure.

This focal-point fountain with its three spouts provides the soothing sounds of running water thanks to access to plumbing lines.

Plumbing for Outdoor Showers

Outdoor showers bring indoor comforts to your deck or patio area and can be installed anywhere if you have the right plumbing and structure.

For infrequent shower use, a hose hooked up to the showerhead may suffice.

For longer (and warmer) soaks, position the shower against a wall of your house, where you can tap into existing plumbing. Each fall be sure to shut off the water supply and drain water from the pipes. To avoid freezing pipes connect underground pipes to a valve box at the back of the shower.

If the shower is positioned away from the house, consider installing a solar water heater rather than a standard hot water line to conserve energy and store hot water.

Consider sink placement: A freestanding outdoor sink requires more sophisticated plumbing than a sink against one wall of the house that taps into existing plumbing.

ELECTRICITY

An outdoor space with adequate electrical service can add to your enjoyment of the area and expand its potential uses. If you typically bring work home from the office or work from home, adequate outdoor electrical outlets mean you can take advantage of pleasant weather without falling behind on necessary tasks.

Having your new outdoor space wired for electricity doesn't have to be all about work either. If you're planning an outdoor kitchen, well-placed electrical outlets can service blenders, rotisseries, and other small appliances. Create a warm ambience for an evening party with festive lamps rated for outdoor use.

Think about how you'll outfit the deck or patio and where furnishings will be placed to best determine locations for outlets. Outdoor receptacles must be protected by a ground fault circuit interrupter and placed in weatherproof boxes that seal out moisture.

If electrical outlets are nearby, you can even hang outdoor lighting from overhead fixtures to create illumination.

Electronics Made for the Outdoors

Electronics aren't just for the indoors. Advancements in speakers and televisions take the meaning of outdoor living to the next level.

Groove to your favorite tunes with speakers made for outdoor use. To maintain a cohesive look, install speakers that blend with your living space. For example, if you have a white overhead structure, look for white speakers. You also can find speakers that resemble rocks and models that can be buried in the ground. Waterproof speakers allow you to integrate sound at your pool or spa.

Catch the big game on a weatherproof television. These units come in a variety of sizes to fit your deck or patio area. If you don't have a weatherproof television, protect your TV by placing it in a weatherproof cabinet. Make sure you get a waterproof remote control too.

LIGHTING

A well-designed outdoor lighting system allows you to use the spaces in comfort and safety even after dark. It should illuminate key areas, such as conversation spots, cooking centers, doors, walkways, pool surrounds, and stairs. It also can be used to highlight special features such as plants or trees and provide security lighting along foundation plantings and fences.

Outdoor Bulb Options

BULB TYPE	DESCRIPTION	PROS	CONS
Incandescent	Most commonly used bulb type.	Casts a warm, pleasant light. Can be dimmed with rheostat switches. Least expensive.	Produces a lot of heat. Can dim with use. Uses a lot of electricity.
Tungsten-Halogen	Low-voltage, pricier type of incandescent bulb that produces an intense burn.	Ideal for accent lighting. Won't dim with age. Can last four times as long as incandescent bulbs. Uses less electricity.	Beams can produce intense heat. Must be used away from flammable materials. Must be handled carefully. Direct contact with skin will contaminate the bulb, damage the glass, and cause it to burn out rapidly.
High-Intensity Discharge (HID)	Includes metal halide, mercury vapor, and high-pressure sodium lamps. Used primarily for safety lighting near pools and illuminating large areas, such as tennis courts.	Reliable, brilliant light. Energy-efficient.	Not recommended for use with dimmer switches. Creates an orange or greenish cast.
Xenon	Brightness of halogen bulb without the intense heat and delicate handling.	Low voltage. Energy-efficient.	Expensive.
Fluorescent	Lasts longer in fixtures that aren't turned off and on frequently. For the most pleasing light quality, look for color-corrected or warm white bulbs.	Budget-savvy choice. Uses just a third of the electricity and costs less over time than incandescent.	Can cast a harsh light. Slow to come to full wattage.
LED (Light Emitting Diode)	Newer lighting device that does not require a heating filament to produce light.	Extremely long-lasting. Dims rather than completely burning out when LED fails. Lights up quickly. Requires less power than incandescent bulbs. Available in a range of colors.	Expensive compared with other types. Not yet as readily available.

Incorporating outdoor lighting into your design requires careful planning. Small lights built into deck stairs enable guests to see where they are stepping.

Path lighting makes walking safe at night. Low decorative fixtures cast light directly on a walkway.

Voltage Options

Outdoor lighting comes in three types: regular fixtures that use 120-volt household current, low-voltage, and solar-power. Low-voltage lighting is increasingly popular because it is safe, inexpensive, and easy to install. Manufacturers of low-voltage lighting offer an array of styles and configurations made especially for outdoor residential use. These are readily available at home improvement centers. Low-voltage and solar lights are freestanding units or can be fastened to posts, railings, stair risers, and other components.

Lighting Techniques

When you plan a lighting scheme, keep the design as flexible as possible so your lighting is appropriate for a variety of uses. Use several circuits and incorporate dimmer switches that allow you to control the amount of light in individual areas. Place switches indoors so you can turn lighting on before venturing into the yard. If you want switches outdoors as well, you'll need to have three-way switches installed.

To avoid glare make sure the light source—the bulb—is hidden from direct view by shades, covers, or plantings; another option is to position the bulb so the light bounces off a large reflective surface such as a wall.

An outdoor lighting system usually combines several lighting techniques. The most common types:

- **Downlighting** is placed on poles, in trees, or on the sides of houses. It shines directly onto surfaces and is used for general illumination and safety.

Small outdoor lights strategically placed among flowerbeds might not provide enough illumination for safe walking after dark, but they do contribute mood lighting.

- **Uplighting** is placed low to the ground and directed upward for dramatic effect and to highlight individual objects such as unusual trees or garden sculptures.
- **Passage lighting** illuminates pathways and stairs. A series of small downlights usually leads the way along a defined route.
- **Area lighting** illuminates large surfaces such as lawns, patios, and decks. Several types of lighting produce an overall effect that is not too harsh or distracting.

Fixture Choices

The right kinds of illumination are key for setting the mood of your space. Do you want lighting that provides elegance, brightens casual celebrations or ensures safety?

Choices for outdoor lighting include chandeliers and sconces, electric or battery-power floor and table lamps, lanterns, battery-charge canister lights, strands of white lights, torches, and candles. Consider access when you select the lighting for an outdoor space. Electric chandeliers, sconces, and floor and table lamps require outlets. Chandeliers also require an overhead structure such as a pergola for mounting.

Small strands of lights beautifully define the perimeter of a rooftop, deck railing, umbrella, or gazebo. Battery-charge or solar-power canister lights work well when lighting a table or lining the walkway. Candles, lanterns, and torches provide romantic light that works anywhere—as long as breezes don't snuff them out.

This carriage lamp could be mounted in any number of places in your outdoor room; in this case it is suspended from a wrought-iron lattice.

Design Tip

Solar-power light fixtures are attractive and versatile—you can set them in spots where you can't install low-voltage lights. Make sure you place solar lights in areas that receive full sun exposure during the day to ensure maximum performance at night. Available in a variety of styles to suit your outdoor decor, solar fixtures can be found at your local home improvement center or other retail stores.

Path lights may operate on a line voltage system; others are solar-power and require no wiring.

Subtle lighting may be added to railings or other deck components. This striking architectural detail is visually interesting and contributes illumination.

FIREPLACES

It's no wonder that fireplaces have become common focal points for outdoor rooms. Their warmth and character light up even the most drab spaces and extend the amount of time you're able to enjoy your patio or deck. Before having an outdoor fireplace installed, make sure local building codes will allow it. If so the options are almost limitless. If you have an interior fireplace with a chimney along an exterior wall, you may be able to situate the outdoor fireplace to share the chimney. Otherwise plan fire placement to maximize its benefits. Make the fireplace the centerpiece of a screen to block unsightly views or use it to delineate an outdoor room.

Group comfortable outdoor furnishings near the fireplace for a natural conversation area. An overhead structure near the fireplace will offer protection for enjoying the warmth of the fire in less than ideal weather. If a permanent fireplace is out of your budget or would overwhelm a small patio, consider a portable fire pit if local codes allow.

Distinguished by different cuts of stone, this stately, old-world fireplace serves as a focal point.

An intimate grouping of chairs in front of a stone fireplace encourages a fireside chat. The covered overhead structure supported by stately columns blocks out rain and harsh sun.

DESIGN GALLERY
Fireplaces

The soft radiance emitted by outdoor fireplaces creates an intimate setting. The key is to choose a striking surround that makes a statement even when it's not lighted. Get in the glow with these ideas.

1: This woodburning fireplace doubles as an entertainment center—behind the cabinet doors lies a flat-panel TV. The fireplace's handsome bluestone detailing echoes the floor.

2: A stately river rock fireplace and fir mantel incorporate the best of nature's bounty. Large niches on each side of the hearth keep firewood close at hand.

3: This slate fireplace surround weaves nature's palette into this outdoor room and complements the style of the nearby outdoor kitchen. A fir-and-steel arbor covered in vines protects the fireplace from the elements.

4: By day this large stone fireplace blends seamlessly with the stone patio and brick walls. At night it sets the space aglow. Two sconces mounted on the fireplace surround provide additional light.

5: A cobalt blue fireplace surround creates a fiesta of color and classic Southwest style.

3

4

5

OUTDOOR KITCHENS

If the kitchen is the heart of the home, why not make an outdoor kitchen the centerpiece of your backyard retreat? Begin by determining how you will use the kitchen. The requirements for the occasional cookout are quite different from full-scale entertaining. Consider your dining style too. The outdoors obviously is ideal for casual gatherings, yet it's possible to create a formal outdoor space suitable for hosting important business affairs. An outdoor kitchen should include areas for cooking, dining, and entertaining. Plan based on needs first then alter to fit the space and your budget. Patios are able to support the weight of even the most elaborate outdoor kitchen. A deck, however, may require additional structural support.

Location

Situate the outdoor kitchen next to the interior kitchen for ease of transferring food. If you're planning a full-service outdoor kitchen, you'll also have easier access to existing plumbing, gas, and electrical lines. Plan shelter for the space. Remember that a grill produces much more heat than a stove, so position the cooking unit in a protected space. An overhead structure enables grilling even in inclement weather.

Amenities

An outdoor kitchen can be as simple as a stand-alone grill or as elaborate as a full-service kitchen with zones for storage, food prep, cooking, dining, and cleanup. In a full kitchen the work areas can include virtually any amenity found in an indoor kitchen including countertops, sink, refrigerator, grill, pizza oven, rotisserie, microwave, cabinetry, and specialized storage. As outdoor kitchens have increased in popularity, manufacturers have responded by designing more elements for use outside. You'll now find cabinetry, fixtures, and an array of appliances specifically for outdoor use.

Design Tip

If you desire an outdoor kitchen, ask yourself a few questions to get the planning process moving. How many people do you expect to entertain regularly? Will you host family and friends or will you entertain for business? Also consider the type of outdoor cooking you do and how often you do it.

This outdoor kitchen positioned against an exterior wall of the home includes a prep sink, an undercounter refrigerator, and an icemaker. The window above the sink serves as a pass-through.

Layout

Your new outdoor kitchen will function best with an efficient layout no matter the size or complexity of the elements you plan to include. Carefully consider grill placement first. If you'll do lots of grilling, think about typical wind patterns. Position the dining table away from where grill smoke will blow.

Then apply the best of indoor kitchen design principles to position the other elements. Group appliances and similar items by function. Include plenty of counterspace for food preparation, with counters on each side of the cooking area if possible. A prep sink with a faucet is useful for cleaning fruits and vegetables and filling pots. It also will simplify cleanup after a meal so dishes can be rinsed before carrying them inside. Include a trash receptacle near the cleanup station.

As with an indoor kitchen, outdoor kitchens function best when there's sufficient space for people to move. To accommodate socializing with friends and family, incorporate a raised bar-height countertop between the kitchen and the rest of the deck or patio. Add seating so guests can visit with the cook during meal prep.

This beautiful cooking station features stonework and beaded board in addition to a full menu of kitchen appliances and amenities.

Tucked against one side of the house, this kitchen is within easy reach of the table and takes advantage of access to the home's plumbing.

Cost Considerations

Outdoor kitchens can dramatically increase the value of your home. The more amenities your kitchen offers, the higher the return on investment. You can score a functional kitchen for as little as $2,000 or as high as $60,000. Here's how:

Standard: If you're looking to stick to a budget, consider a basic setup with a stainless-steel grill, an undercounter refrigerator, and storage space. An additional $1,000 yields a bar sink, patio umbrella, and cast-aluminum table and chairs.

Luxurious: If you plan to go all out, your fully covered, high-tech kitchen should boast a multitasking grill with a rotisserie and side burners, weather-resistant cabinetry, and appliances such as a sink, dishwasher, microwave, and refrigerator. To enhance the high-profile look, plan to invest in a fireplace, wrought-iron table and chairs, and bar-height stools.

Adequate counterspace is essential for food preparation especially when you're making an entire meal outdoors. Make sure you have at least 18 to 24 inches of countertop on each side of the sink for washing, cutting, and setting food.

DESIGN GALLERY

Outdoor Kitchens

One of the biggest trends in outdoor living, alfresco kitchens dish up a hearty helping of amenities to flavor your dining needs. Customize your outdoor kitchen with these suggestions.

1: Tiling the surface next to your grill allows for convenient food preparation—and subtle splashes of color, as this durable tile countertop proves.

2: Develop a color scheme to express your style. Bold blue paint punches up the cabinetry while the playful yellow-and-blue tile countertop extends up the backsplash.

3: If alfresco cooking is a favorite activity, consider investing in a multitasking grilling island with amenities such as ample counterspace and side burners.

4: Storage is an essential element of an outdoor kitchen—and it needn't look utilitarian. This handsome white cabinet door glides open to reveal a deep sliding shelf.

5: A stacked-stone grill surround helps this outdoor cooking area blend in with the patio.

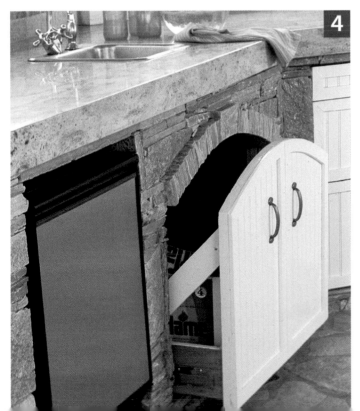

Large boulders and a combination of evergreen trees, shrubs, perennials, and ornamental grasses give this freeform pool a formal look.

SPAS & POOLS

Recent trends have taken pools and spas to a whole new level of relaxation and style. The once-standard rectangular pool surrounded by a gray concrete slab is more the exception than the rule. Pools and spas often have organic shapes with patio or deck surrounds that mirror the curves and gentle edges. Start your pool or spa plan by looking to your house. Note the features that define your home's style such as its overall shape, exterior surface treatments, colors, and materials. Use these as a guide when selecting the shapes, finishes, colors, and details for your pool, the deck or patio, and the surrounding landscape. If your home is formal, consider a linear pool shape with a brick or stone tile patio surround. If your house boasts a more rustic style, choose an organic pool shape and a deck or freeform flagstone patio.

Allow plenty of space around the pool or spa. You'll probably spend even more time out of the water than in it so include ample surface area for furnishings. Set aside room for poolside lounging but also carve out spaces for conversation groupings and outdoor dining. If the pool will be a spot for frequent entertaining, you'll want even more space than if it will function solely as a family retreat.

A wooden pergola shades this poolside deck and creates a cool space for kicking back after a long swim. The rich hue of the pergola and deck warms up the neutral pool surround.

With multiple distinct areas for dining and lounging, this spacious multilevel patio encourages poolside relaxation.

163

Surfaces

Take care when selecting the surface that will surround your pool or spa. Not only must it stand up to splashes and potential standing water, but safety also is key. The surface should not get slippery when exposed to water and must remain free of rough edges, popped fasteners, splinters, and anything else that might hurt bare feet. Opt for light-color surfaces that won't absorb as much heat and will stay cooler than dark ones.

Structures

Overhead structures provide relief from the sun. A poolside patio or deck will get hot even when you carefully select surface materials, and although a dip in the water will provide relief, you want to enjoy your backyard retreat when you're out of the water too. Create a plan for shaded areas. Arbors and pergolas provide shade and can be designed in styles that complement the look of your home, pool, and landscaping. Awnings that attach to the house can be extended when you want shade and retracted when you don't. See pages 96 and 134 for more information about overhead structures and creating shade.

Privacy is another critical component for a pool or spa area. Building codes in most areas require a fence around a pool. But

Hidden by an Arts and Crafts-style fence, this soothing spa is a haven for relaxation. The pool's slate coping and a soft gray interior create a modern aesthetic.

Shimmering water splashes over this stone border, creating an iridescent effect. Pools with gray bottoms give water a crystal blue look.

Use unusual elements to distinguish your pool from the rest of the landscape. For example, this concrete urn formally announces the entrance to the pool area.

An abundance of low, upright, and drooping plants combine in this gardenlike setting. Peeking out from the plantings, small statues add a playful element.

Design Tip

A natural-look pool creates a resortlike escape even if you live in a residential area. Surround your pool with natural materials such as wood or stone and line the area around the pool with showy planting beds to bring the beauty of the garden poolside. For extra style consider adding a fountain that spills water into the pool—the sounds and ambience it creates will rival that of a waterfall.

depending on the location of your property and the fence, there may not be as much privacy as you'd like. Adding screens in strategic spots helps create an intimate spot for a spa. Plants can provide privacy without making you feel fenced in.

Integrating **storage** with your deck or patio will help contain the plethora of pool cleaning supplies, accessories, and toys you may have. Include hinged tops on built-in benches to maximize space. If you have young children, keep chemicals in a locked compartment.

DESIGN GALLERY
Spas & Pools

Make a splash with your spa and pool design. Natural materials and a little creativity can transform a standard spa or pool into a stunning water feature. Take a dip with these ideas.

1: Structured wood deck panels and stone pavers blend gracefully to create a poolscape with a visually appealing blend of colors and textures.

2: A stone wall adds interesting texture and serves as a border between a shapely pool and the landscape. The fountain and colorful flowers soften the transition from wall to pool.

3: Bold color—in the form of blue ceramic tiles—gives this pool its signature style. The pool boasts a raised spa and several small fountains that spout cascading water.

4: A stacked-stone surround encircles this spa and establishes visual harmony with the existing landscape. Shallow stone steps lead to a small sitting area that's perfect for enjoying the view.

5: Built into the first level of this Western red cedar deck, a hot tub awards spectacular views. Its curvy form perfectly hugs the shapely deck.

PATHS & WALKWAYS

An inviting walkway from your new deck or patio through the yard opens the entire landscape to the possibilities of outdoor living. Look to existing traffic patterns through the yard to determine best placement. It's a good idea to lay out your path before purchasing materials—a garden hose works well to delineate the sides of the path during planning stages. The walkway can be as freeform as you

Loosely winding through a formal garden, evenly spaced pavers gracefully ascend to shallow stairs leading to adjacent pool and pavilion areas.

This bluestone pathway passes through a double gate on the way to a backyard sanctuary. Bluestone stores heat, making it pleasant for bare feet even on cool nights.

like but plan to make your path at least 36 inches wide so two people can walk comfortably side by side.

Materials

Brick paths exude an old-world charm that complements most houses and landscaping styles. A brick walkway can take almost any shape, from a straight formal walk to a meandering path. The many patterns that can be created with brick further expand your options.

Flagstone walkways add style and timeless beauty. Adjustable to virtually any shape or configuration, flagstone softens the straight lines of an otherwise geometric landscape. Because each flagstone can vary in thickness, adjust the depth of the base to level the surface for easier walking.

Loose materials—including small river rocks, crushed stone, and gravel—make interesting paths that add a soft crunch underfoot as you walk. Though loose materials tend to be informal, you can change the character of the path with the type of loose material and edging you choose.

Deck paving materials offer another walkway option. A wooden plank walkway, for example, is an ideal way to lead from an attached deck at the house to a platform deck in the yard. The decking will be exposed to ground moisture so be sure to use pressure-treated or other moisture-resistant lumber.

Mix materials for interest. For example, combine brick and stone tiles to create a patchwork effect. Juxtaposing two elements in the same pathway is one way to bring visual unity to disparate materials used elsewhere in the landscape.

Destinations

Plan small surprises along your path rather than paving a straight walk. Curves are a cue to slow down and enjoy the view. Instead of bringing visitors straight from the yard to the patio or deck, plan a path that takes a slightly circuitous route, offering unexpected views of the garden along the way.

Consider making your walkway extra roomy. For interest broaden the walk at curves and flare it at both ends. Add a bench at a wide portion of the path to encourage lingering. Or widen one end of the path for a visual effect of greater or lesser distance.

Though flowers abound, these tidy plantings keep the brick walkway fully accessible.

Design Tip

Illuminating paths and walkways ensures safety when walking at night. Path lights enhance your overall lighting plan and add a dose of style to your outdoor spaces. These fixtures come in a variety of styles; choose a style that fits the mood of your outdoor space. For example hanging carriage lights work along a formal path while sleek solar units fit better in a more contemporary scheme.

A rustic flagstone path is the perfect choice to weave through a secluded courtyard filled with drought-tolerant plants.

CHAPTER 7

Incorporate Landscaping

Integrating with Landscaping, Assessing Landscaping Needs,
Foundation Plantings

No outdoor living space is complete without the addition of lush landscaping. Boasting a pleasing tapestry of colors and textures, landscaping blurs the distinction between your outdoor living space and the surrounding yard. In this chapter you'll learn to effectively integrate landscaping into your deck or patio design. Create four-season interest with plants that easily adapt to your climate whether you live in the Southwest or Northeast. Discover how to soften hard surfaces with well-placed foundation plants.

INTEGRATING WITH LANDSCAPING

Your new deck or patio should provide a pleasing transition between your house and the surrounding landscape. As such the structure should complement the colors, shape, and style of the house. Likewise the landscaping—plants, trees, shrubs, vines, and other features—should enhance the deck or patio. The most successful results typically occur when significant landscaping features are integrated with deck or patio plans at the beginning of the process.

Do your best to protect plants, shrubs, and trees as you create the plan for your outdoor spaces. For example a deck can be designed to accommodate a mature tree rather than having it removed. Let design professionals and contractors know that you want these features preserved. If possible footings for decks should be placed outside a tree's drip line to prevent root damage.

Think of plants as design elements that will enhance your outdoor room just as furnishings, accessories, and art enhance indoor spaces. Select colors, textures, and forms that work with your house and patio or deck. Buy multiples of each plant for pleasing repetition throughout the landscape.

Defined by beds and planters, this landscape creates a striking view that can be enjoyed indoors and out. The arrangement of the plants enlivens the house without overwhelming it.

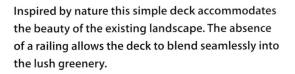

Design Tip

Eyecatching container gardens lend a welcome burst of color to the landscape—and they're easy to create. The key is creativity. Experiment with different plant color and texture combinations and display your creations in showy containers. Just be sure to group plants with similar growing needs and use a lightweight potting mix that drains quickly but retains moisture.

Inspired by nature this simple deck accommodates the beauty of the existing landscape. The absence of a railing allows the deck to blend seamlessly into the lush greenery.

Raised flowerbeds outline this deck. The planters echo the deck design and provide seasonal color.

ASSESSING LANDSCAPING NEEDS

The right landscaping can help the function as well as the aesthetics of your new outdoor room. Large deciduous trees are one of the best sources of summertime shade. Tall evergreens provide screening when positioned near an otherwise exposed patio or deck. Plant flowering vines where they can climb an overhead structures and by summer you'll have a lush, perhaps fragrant, source of shade. If you plan a deck that will cantilever over a steeply sloped yard, the right landscaping can minimize runoff under the structure.

In addition to picking the right plants to enhance your enjoyment of an outdoor space, select the best plants for your climate to minimize care. If you have a shady yard, choose full-shade plants that will thrive in that environment. If your outdoor space will bask in full sun, select sun-loving plants that benefit from soaking up the rays. When possible plant with native species. It's a growing trend for good reason. Native species require less water than other plants and therefore benefit the environment. Native plants also typically withstand pests better and tend to thrive with less care.

A mix of tall and medium-height trees and shrubs serves as natural walls for this open arbor, *right*, creating cool shade on hot summer afternoons.

Perennials surrounding the deck contribute season-long greenery while a bevy of blooming plants in pots and window boxes puts on a show of pink and purple flowers.

Landscaping Poolside

Landscaping can take an ordinary pool surround from drab to fab. Visually connect your yard and pool with these poolscaping suggestions:

Stagger container gardens around the pool. Not only will you infuse your pool with color, but you also can easily move the planters if you need to keep an eye on kids.

Generate shade and privacy with midsize plants. Avoid large plants, which can hinder accessibility.

Select plants with soft, rounded edges that won't poke you as you move about.

Create visual interest with large rocks or waterfalls.

FOUNDATION PLANTINGS

Shrubs and other vertical plants positioned at the base of a raised deck help visually connect the yard and the structure. Foundation plants conceal the support structure of the deck to place the focus on the overall outdoor living space. The best designs feature a gentle cascade of plants with the tallest in the back, gradually transitioning to low groundcover in the front.

Expand outdoor living space by integrating a raised deck, foundation plantings, stairways, and patios. Include patios and paths at yard level. Leave space between the patios and the deck for foundation plantings that will ease the vertical transition between spaces. For a landscape that will really wow, consider a small waterfall that flows from deck level to a lower patio level.

Design Tip

A tree or shrub can wear out its welcome if it consumes your deck or patio. That's why it's important to check plant tags for the expected mature height and width before purchasing new shrubs and trees. Though they look petite at the nursery, they might overtake their intended space and obstruct good views. To ensure a good fit for your space, look for dwarf varieties.

This deck is divided into sections, but the foundation plantings—including small trees, low-maintenance shrubs, and playful beds—weave a unified look throughout.

DESIGN GALLERY
Landscaping

When you landscape you infuse your outdoor space with nature's bounty. Here are some ways to design a landscape that mingles effortlessly with your deck or patio.

1: Native plants fill a garden that's high on style and low on maintenance. This garden also incorporates ornamental grasses and perennials.

2: A lush surround of groundcover, ferns, Japanese maples, and evergreens lends an almost secluded feel to this deck even though it's only steps from the house.

3: Break up large expanses of plantings with an attractive pot. To show off a planter's design, grow tall, spiky grasses that draw the eye.

4: Drought-tolerant plants create a lush-looking landscape in dry climates and minimize care and watering needs.

5: Plantings of all shapes and sizes can supplement fences and screens for privacy.

6: With showy plumes of ornamental grasses and small jewellike blossoms, this poolside planting bed evokes an oasis.

CHAPTER 8

Furnish the Space

Outdoor Decorating Basics, Color & Texture,
Outdoor Furniture, Fabrics, Accessories

An empty patio or deck is like a blank canvas waiting to be turned into a masterpiece. The furnishings you add complete the transformation and reflect your style, whether it's classic or quirky. Outdoor decor can fill your deck or patio with the comforts of home and brighten the look of the existing hardscape. In this chapter you'll learn to integrate color and texture, choose outdoor furniture that enhances comfort yet stands up to the elements, and dress up your space with lively fabrics. As you examine outdoor furnishings, remember to add accents such as plants or decorative tile for a final flourish.

OUTDOOR DECORATING BASICS

Outdoor living is all about creating a relaxed environment you enjoy. Though a new deck or patio alone will start you in the right direction, the true comforts come after you've outfitted the space with furnishings and accessories ideal for the activities that will take place in your new outdoor room. To make the most of outdoor decorating, consider how you will use the space then decorate to fit its intended function and your lifestyle. Be bold and creative, if you like, while at the same time strive to create a cohesive, unified design.

Start with one or two key furnishings. Maybe you've found the perfect dining table or a chaise longue where you plan to while away the summer. Build the rest of your decor around that item. To be most comfortable in your lounge chair, you'll probably want a side table close at hand to hold reading materials and a beverage. When you entertain guests will need suitable seating for conversation so add comfortable coordinating chairs. A dining table with an umbrella and chairs is another smart addition. Then complete the space with pillows, lighting, and accessories.

Groupings of furnishings, rich fabrics, artwork arranged on the walls, and various forms of lighting segment this courtyard into a series of rooms.

Simple, stylish patio furniture offers comfort and directs attention to the focal point fountain.

COLOR & TEXTURE

Whether your goal is to create a lively outdoor party zone or a quiet place of solitude, color and texture are important parts of the equation. Color affects mood. Red, for example, creates excitement and energy while green is associated with relaxation and calm. Because your new patio or deck probably will be surrounded, at least in part, by a swath of green lawn or potted plants, play with color on your new structure to create the environment you desire. Warm colors tend to make a space feel cozier and more intimate while cool colors make it seem more spacious and airy.

There are lots of starting points for choosing color. Thanks to enhancements in outdoor fabrics, you'll have a variety of colors and textures from which to select. Your favorite color may provide the perfect beginning. Or take a cue from your house and introduce more saturated hues of existing colors to enliven your outdoor space while maintaining a cohesive look. If your house is contemporary, look for industrial colors including cool grays, deep purples, metallics, and classic black and whites. For a more traditional look, white wicker never goes out of style. Gardens provide another inspiration for color. Look to your favorite flowers for hues to use in seat cushions, umbrellas, or awnings and pick accent colors that complement your favorites. Or use color to start a new design theme that matches the style you envision for your new outdoor space. Citrus and water hues are popular and can help set the tone for a tropical hideaway—even if your deck or patio is in the heartland.

For even more visual interest, think texture. The largest texture in your space probably will be the surface of your deck or patio. But don't limit yourself to just one texture. Heighten interest by mixing things up. Look for bamboo, stone, wood, wicker, and other natural textures as foundation pieces. Then introduce softer touches with fabrics for furnishings, umbrellas, pillows, and throws.

Saturated hues—from citrus fruits to the pillows—combine with the fireplace to generate warmth. The canopy of trees and hanging baskets create a casual atmosphere.

Enhancing Natural Beauty

Use these elements to achieve an outdoor living space that blends seamlessly with nature:

Colors. Incorporate nature's extensive palette—leafy green, sky blue, and more—into your outdoor living space. To complete the cohesive look, paint the exterior of your house in earthy hues.

Floors. Use natural materials such as wood or stone to line the "floors" of your deck or patio. To delineate seating areas use throw rugs made of durable, natural fibers.

Furnishings and accessories. Opt for furnishings made of wood or wicker. Punctuate your space with accents made from natural materials such as stone or terra-cotta.

Lights. Install low-wattage outdoor lights to provide a soft glow that takes a backseat to starry skies without compromising safety.

Water. Stimulate relaxation with a fountain or birdbath that provides soothing sounds.

Large containers
of purple petunias
form the backdrop
for furnishings
adorned with splashy
throw pillows.

OUTDOOR FURNITURE

Outdoor furnishings are more comfortable, durable, and varied than ever. While that means you have plenty of options, once again function is key. You want outdoor furnishings that suit how you'll use the space and your lifestyle.

Collections

Many companies offer a variety of furniture pieces in collections that make it easy to coordinate various items. Options include sling furniture, deep seating, modular furniture, and chat-height furniture with lower and wider chairs and tables. Consider how you'll use your outdoor space and select furnishings that coincide. If you have multiple outdoor rooms, going with a collection—or at least selecting various pieces with the same finish—can help pull together the entire space.

Materials

Natural materials including wicker, twig, and rattan have been outdoor mainstays for years. Although they're not weather-resistant, they're durable enough to withstand protected outdoor use. Wood furniture constructed from teak, redwood, or cypress is weather- and rot-resistant so it's safe to leave on an uncovered patio or deck. Natural wood weathers to a silvery gray. Furniture-grade pine, fir, and oak require annual coats of stain or sealer to keep them at their best in the elements.

Metal furnishings range from the lightweight, rustproof, and durable cast or wrought aluminum to the classic, heavy cast or wrought iron. Iron will require periodic touch-ups as it is prone to rust.

Synthetic furniture includes a range of options from inexpensive, stackable chairs to heavy-duty plastic that

A bow-shape hammock creates a striking statement on a simple, secluded patio.

Adirondack chairs drenched in bright hues are the focal point of this patio. A fresh coat of paint is an inexpensive way to spice up wood furniture.

These brown wicker chairs complement the home's earthy palette and rich textures.

Furniture Sizing for Outdoor Rooms

FURNISHING TYPE	MINIMUM SQUARE FOOTAGE REQUIRED	IDEAL SQUARE FOOTAGE FOR COMFORT
36-inch round table and four chairs	A square or circle 9 feet across, a total of 80–90 square feet	A square or circle 12 feet across, a total of 140–150 square feet
48-inch round table and six chairs	A square or circle 10 feet across, a total of 100–110 square feet	A square or circle 13 feet across, a total of 160–180 square feet
Adirondack chair	A rectangle 6 feet long and 3.5 feet wide, a total of 21 square feet	A rectangle 8 feet long and 4 feet wide, a total of 32 square feet
Freestanding hammock with self-supporting stand	A rectangle 9 feet long and 6 feet wide, a total of 54 square feet	A rectangle 9×6-feet, 3 feet at each side for clearance, a total of 108 square feet
Built-in bench seat 6 feet long	A rectangle 6 feet wide with 3 feet of clearance in front of the bench plus a bench depth of 18 inches, a total of 27 square feet	A rectangle 6 feet wide with 5 feet of clearance in front of the bench plus a bench depth of 18 inches, a total of 39 square feet

Weatherproof materials are a must when furniture such as these chaise longues meant for sunbathing are exposed to the elements.

Design Tip

Your ultimate goal when arranging outdoor furniture should be to establish a comfortable and accessible space. Arrange tables and chairs in ways that stimulate conversation—especially if you plan to entertain. If your deck or patio area is large enough, include multiple groupings of furniture—perhaps one for dining and another for chatting—to emulate different functional areas inside the home.

A dining table with a large umbrella and matching chair cushions takes center stage on this stone patio. Coordinating chairs and end tables scattered about the patio provide other spots for sitting.

looks like wood but doesn't require the maintenance. Synthetic wicker offers the classic looks of real wicker but is moistureproof.

Eco-friendly outdoor furniture is becoming more widely available as green living goes mainstream. Look for pieces made from reclaimed or sustainable-harvest wood, recycled plastic, recycled wrought iron, and more.

Shapes and Sizes

In general a number of smaller furnishings work better than one large piece. A grouping of chairs can be rearranged to suit an intimate gathering or a large party. Dining tables come in a variety of shapes and sizes. Round tables are ideal for encouraging lively conversation because it's possible to see everyone seated. Small tables typically seat four while larger ones comfortably seat six. For more formal dinners long rectangular tables are available.

Or for more flexibility consider purchasing several smaller square tables that can be pushed together to seat a large group. Allow plenty of surface space for furnishings. The chart on page 185 provides some basic recommendations.

FABRICS

For a deck or patio space that's as comfortable as your indoor rooms, select fabrics that complement the look of the outdoor room, coordinate with the style of the furnishings, and fit your style. Manufacturers that specialize in outdoor fabrics now offer a plethora of colors, patterns, and specialty weaves that are nearly as soft and comfortable as those for indoors. To simplify decorating look for color families with coordinating prints and solids. Use fabric outdoors to cover cushions and pillows. To create a more sheltered deck or patio, select fabrics for draperies and canopies as well. For special occasions add color with floor coverings and tablecloths.

Most outdoor fabrics resist damage from fading and staining. Natural fabrics are least resistant to mold and mildew so choose synthetic fabrics that replicate the look and feel of natural fibers but are less likely to suffer from mold and mildew or to fade. To extend the life of pillows and cushions sporting any type of fabric, stow them when not in use. Even if the fabric is weather-resistant, the padding is less able to withstand moisture.

Soft green cushions paired with accent pillows in coordinating hues and patterns put this seating arrangement in the limelight.

Look to plant life for fabric inspiration. These pink, green, and white striped pillows match the large pot of caladiums.

Design Tip

Weave fabrics with rich colors and textures into your outdoor space. Line chairs with colorful pillows and top tables with pretty cloths. Replace side tables with fabric-covered ottomans and fasten sheer fabric to an overhead structure for outdoor drapery. Use weatherproof outdoor fabric or to save money make pillows, tablecloths, and drapes from leftover fabric—just be sure to store indoors when not in use.

Mixing and matching fabrics infuses this small space with personality. These Moroccan-inspired rugs and throws evoke an eclectic ambience.

A sugar-kettle fountain encircled with hummingbird plant, verbena, caladium, and agapanthus serves up splashy style and soothing sounds.

ACCESSORIES

The most successful spaces are those filled with things you love. That goes for a patio or deck as much as it does for an interior room. A walk through the outdoor living and gardening aisles of virtually any store provides a bevy of options. The decks and patios featured in this book should offer the inspiration for using those objects.

Bring nature onto the deck or patio with lush plants in containers that complement your decor. Small tabletop water features deliver soothing sounds right to you. Include candles in tabletop arrangements for evening dining and throughout the space for an inviting overall glow. For a special event stage flowers cut from the garden in vases on tabletops, walls, and shelves. Display accessories throughout the space. If your yard is lacking vertical structures, sculptures can help to define outdoor rooms. Group small whimsical outdoor accessories such as birdhouses, watering cans, rocks, or shells for more visual impact than a single small item. Wall art helps break up the expanse of a fence or lattice screen—decorative tiles, architectural salvage, and stone carvings are weather-resistant options.

An intricately framed mirror, *above*, adds an unexpected touch of elegance to an outdoor wall.

Small decorative items such as this cobalt blue planter, *below*, pack a major punch when placed on a deck or patio.

A trip to the flea market can yield a treasure trove of outdoor accessories. These vintage finds, *above*, accentuate a privacy fence and are accompanied by a pair of blooming hanging baskets.

DESIGN GALLERY
Outdoor Furnishings

Just as indoor spaces benefit from carefully selected furnishings and fabrics so do outdoor rooms. These attractive, weather-resistant fabrics and furnishings create cozy, carefree outdoor living spaces.

1: Painting an iron table and chairs a primary hue punctuates a small patio with visual interest. Mildew-resistant fabrics come in a variety of energetic patterns—these striped pillows fit perfectly with the seating arrangement.

2: Cushioned benches pair with a small folding table to form a seating area on a platform deck. Teak and mahogany are low- or no-maintenance options for outdoor furnishings.

3: A natural wood table set with colorful dishes and matching chairs decorated with playful pillows enhance a setting for family dining.

4: Bright chairs play off bold plant combinations in this small seating area. The fabric on the modern folding chairs is easily removed for storage away from the elements.

5: Sometimes unadorned patio furnishings are all that's needed. The crosshatch pattern on this iron chair adds subtle detail.

CHAPTER 9

Final Considerations

Project Timeline, Project Completion Checklist, Case Studies

As you proceed with your project, remember these final words of wisdom: Planning is the most essential ingredient in constructing your dream deck or patio regardless of whether you do the project yourself or bring in professional help. In this chapter you'll find a handy project timeline and project checklist to guide your progress and help you stay on track. Gain inspiration from case studies of three types of outdoor living spaces to finalize the decisionmaking process and give you peace of mind that you're designing a deck or patio that accommodates your wallet, schedule, and lifestyle.

PROJECT TIMELINE

It's difficult to create a general timeline for an entire deck or patio project because each will vary in length depending on the complexity of the project, the size of the deck or patio, materials and construction methods, available funding, and the challenges presented by the current landscape. This project timeline is designed only to provide an idea of how much time the initial steps leading to the installation may take and to help you keep track of the steps involved in the actual project.

Comprehensive planning went into designing this deck, which features a hot tub, flower boxes, an intricate railing system, and painted squares.

Step 1: (4 weeks)

PREPLANNING*

- ☐ Collect ideas
- ☐ Assess your needs
- ☐ Identify any problems with the existing landscape
- ☐ Develop a budget
- ☐ Identify financing options
- ☐ Identify possible contractors

Step 2: (4–8 weeks)

SELECTION OF PROFESSIONALS

- ☐ Request bids from contractors
- ☐ Determine financing
- ☐ Select and hire a contractor

Step 3: (2–6 weeks)

DESIGN DEVELOPMENT

- ☐ Learn building code requirements
- ☐ Create a rough plan
- ☐ Discuss and refine plan with a design professional
- ☐ Approve design plan and sign design agreement

Step 4: (2–4 weeks)

PRECONSTRUCTION

- ☐ Select products
- ☐ Obtain permits if necessary
- ☐ Prepare calendar of work, material ordering, and inspections
- ☐ Order materials
- ☐ Prepare yard for construction and installation

Step 5: (1–6 weeks)

CONSTRUCTION

- ☐ Complete yard prep if necessary
- ☐ Install deck support structure or base for patio
- ☐ Install decking or patio paving materials
- ☐ Do any additional finishing

Step 6: (1–3 weeks)

FINAL STEPS

- ☐ Inspect the job
- ☐ Ensure everything is to code
- ☐ Obtain the final inspection certificate
- ☐ Make any final payments for materials or services
- ☐ Decorate, landscape, accessorize, and enjoy your new outdoor living space

*The preplanning stage takes an estimated four weeks. For some people, however, this step alone might take a year or more to complete. Many homeowners begin collecting deck and patio ideas years before they even consider undertaking a project. Only you can know when the timing is right to move past the initial idea phase of the project.

Completing a complex project such as this Arts and Crafts-inspired pergola and hot tub surround that combines detailed woodwork with brick may require a generous timeline.

PROJECT COMPLETION CHECKLIST

Because decks and patios are fairly common do-it-yourself projects, use this checklist to keep your job on task.

PLANNING	BUILDING COMPONENTS	FINISHING COMPONENTS
☐ Does the deck or patio provide enough space for planned outdoor activities?	☐ Lumber for deck substructure or gravel patio base	☐ Finishes such as sealer, stain, or paint depending on project plans and materials
☐ If a variety of activities is planned, does the deck or patio offer separate functional areas?	☐ Boards for decking or paving material for patio surface	☐ Outdoor lighting
☐ Does the deck or patio provide enough space for furnishings conducive to planned outdoor activities?	☐ Materials for built-ins such as benches, planters, and storage	☐ Plants, shrubs, trees, and vines used to landscape the finished outdoor structure
☐ Does the deck or patio account for the special features— outdoor kitchen, fireplace, spa, pool, gazebo, etc.—you desire?	☐ Railings—posts, balusters, top rails—for a deck	☐ Furnishings
☐ Does the deck or patio comply with local building codes and zoning ordinances? If required are inspections scheduled on the project plan?	☐ Stairway parts—stringers, risers, treads—for a deck	☐ Accessories
☐ Will it be easy to access the deck or patio from the house?	☐ Edging for a patio if necessary	☐ Freestanding storage components
☐ Will traffic flow naturally from the house to the deck or patio?	☐ Fasteners for a deck	
☐ Will traffic flow naturally through the deck or patio?	☐ Grout or mortar for a patio if necessary	
☐ Is it easy to access the yard from the deck or patio?	☐ Other general materials specific to your project such as skirting for a deck and landscape fabric to block weeds	
☐ Will at least a portion of the deck or patio be shaded during peak use times?	☐ Specific materials for special features including an outdoor kitchen, outdoor shower, spa, pool, gazebo, and screened areas	
☐ If privacy is a concern, are elements such as screens, fences, walls, or tall evergreens part of the plan?		
☐ Are there convenient storage elements for stowing items when not in use?		
☐ Have you budgeted for all project components?		

With a detailed project such as this that involves laying precise brickwork and building large structures, it's important to proceed with each step in an orderly fashion. That way if one problem arises it won't cause other problems later.

CASE STUDIES

Three outdoor rooms, one theme: Though each of these spaces boasts unique characteristics, they all mix function with flair and prove that it's possible to design an outdoor room that's tailored to your time, budget, and needs.

Consider these the good, better, and best of outdoor rooms—from budget-friendly materials to lavish details, they offer something for everyone. Whether you closely identify with one style or would like to combine different elements of each, look to these decks for inspiration when planning your outdoor room.

PAGE 200

PAGE 202

PAGE 204

This deck transforms an awkward-shape yard into a haven for outdoor relaxation. Container plantings infuse the plain wood with bursts of color.

A simple lattice screen above the railing offers privacy for alfresco dining while the narrow shelf aids food prep. To create a similar privacy screen, simply make the frame for the lattice and trim the lattice to fit.

Living Large

With spacesaving design and smart built-in amenities, this deck proves that a small yard can't dash your dreams of comfortable outdoor living.

The deck, which hugs the width of the narrow yard, owes its spaciousness to the open floor plan that can accommodate large gatherings: As many as 30 people can mix and mingle. Though the deck doesn't have a full outdoor kitchen, it boasts ample room for a grill, handy built-in shelves for food prep, and a wooden dining table. A large built-in bench, distinguished by plush cushions and armrests, adds to the inviting atmosphere.

A lattice roof provides a sense of enclosure yet allows sun and shade to reach the space. It also enables comfortable grilling even when rain threatens; a tarp can be spread on the overhead section above the grill.

Lattice screens and arborvitae provide much-needed privacy from the close neighboring houses. Mitered edges round out the deck, giving it a polished look.

Built-in benches and a wooden table make this a perfect spot to enjoy an early-morning cup of coffee.

The overhead structure connects with the house on top of the roof rather than underneath the eaves. This allows for a higher ceiling that still accommodates the height and pitch of the roof.

This charming armrest provides a place to set items without consuming precious floor space. Integrated cupholders prevent wet glasses from damaging the wood.

Victorian Revival

Punctuated by ornate detailing and showy plants, this two-level deck and connecting outdoor room exude classic Victorian style.

Detailed decks such as this require careful planning and attention to detail. The general layout of the main deck area looks simple, but the multiple levels and crisp white railing complete with carved balusters and ball-top finials required skill to complete. The rich decking installed in

an interesting pattern infuses the space with warmth while the Mariposa slate-covered bottom step adds intricate detail and visually connects the structure to the landscape.

The flowers, trees, and shrubs surrounding the deck provide natural boundaries for an outdoor dining room on a nearby stone patio, providing yet another intimate spot to linger in this outdoor haven.

Similar architectural details help this deck look like a natural extension of the home. The two-level structure combines separate areas for dining and relaxation.

A striking combination of red cedar, Alaskan cedar, and redwood provides a warm contrast against the white railings and landscaping. The decking is applied in a herringbone pattern.

The 200 exquisitely crafted balusters on this deck were custom made. Potted plants enhance the Victorian appeal.

Plants of different sizes and colors enclose this corner making a private retreat for dining, *above*. The simple wood table focuses attention on the plants while the pavers informally mingle with thyme for a romantic look and fresh scent.

As the different sizes of shoes illustrate, the new outdoor space provides fun for family members of all ages, *right*. Though the decking pattern isn't from the Victorian era, it blends with the deck's classic style.

Lamps inside the house help light the patio. Though the outdoor area boasts several lighting fixtures, the illumination is soft to create an enjoyable—not glaring—effect. In addition to casting a soft glow, the fire pit offers a warm spot for gathering.

Gracious Glow

By day this spacious deck and patio combination exudes hospitality with its multiple sitting areas, lush landscaping, and comfortable furnishings. As nighttime descends the space still extends a warm welcome thanks to its abundance of strategically placed landscape lighting. Regardless of the size of your outdoor living space, light goes a long way toward creating an inviting atmosphere.

The deck and patio design takes advantage of the home's elegant architecture. A large second-story balcony provides a bird's-eye view of the surrounding scenery. Defined by stately concrete pillars, the patio underneath provides space for intimate fireside conversation. Built onto the lower-level deck, an elaborate gazebo echoes the home's architecture and provides another covered outdoor area for use night or day.

A generous mix of natural materials ties the outdoor living areas together. Wood, stone, and greenery play off of each other to create a harmonious look that's enhanced by the soft lighting.

Simple landscaping ensures that attention remains on the backyard's beautiful structures, which blend with the scale of the home.

Strands of small lights along the gazebo's roofline, paired with lights built into the steps, Illuminate the area around the gazebo, making it functional and elegant at all hours.

Encircled by a stacked-stone surround, the fire pit generates a soft glow day and night. Cushioned wicker chairs, gracefully adorned with sumptuous pillows and throws, provide a sense of comfortable luxury.

Even when the light is off, this stylish fixture provides design impact on the deck.

CHAPTER 10

Resources

Resource Guide, Glossary, Index

Planning and finishing a deck or patio that meets your needs—and includes the features you desire—requires carefully working through numerous steps and making important decisions. Depending on how extensive your project will be, you may want to involve professionals in some or all phases of the project. Listed on the following page are names and contact information for some of the associations and organizations involved in deck and patio design projects. Turn to these groups, in addition to local resources, for assistance. You'll also find a list of terms common to deck and patio projects. Though you don't need to be an expert in the terminology, familiarity with these words and their meanings will allow you to communicate more clearly with professionals.

RESOURCE GUIDE

Professional Organizations

American Homeowners Foundation
6776 Little Falls Rd.
Arlington, VA 22213
800/489-7776   www.americanhomeowners.org

The American Institute of Architects (AIA)
1735 New York Ave. NW
Washington, DC 20006
202/626-7300   800/242-3837   www.aia.org

American Society of Landscape Architects (ASLA)
636 Eye St. NW
Washington, DC 20001
202/898-2444   www.asla.org

PLANET (Professional Landcare Network)
950 Herndon Pkwy., Suite 450
Herndon, VA 20170
800/395-2522   www.landcarenetwork.org

National Association of Home Builders (NAHB)
1201 15th St. NW
Washington, DC 20005
202/266-8200 x 0   800/368-5242   www.nahb.org

National Association
of the Remodeling Industry (NARI)
780 Lee St., Suite 200
Des Plaines, IL 60016
800/611-6274   www.nari.org

American Lighting Association
P.O. Box 420288
Dallas, TX 75342
800/274-4484   www.americanlightingassoc.com

ENERGY STAR
1200 Pennsylvania Ave. NW
Washington, DC 20460
888/782-7937   www.energystar.gov

North American Deck and Railing Association
P.O. Box 829
Quakertown, PA 18951
888/623-7248   www.nadra.org

Contributors and Professionals

Pages 12, 34, 37, 46, 59, 87 (top right), 87 (bottom right)
Photographer: David McDonald

Pages 48 (top), 75 (top), 133 (bottom right)
Photographer: Michael Thompson

Pages 26 (bottom), 61 (bottom), 65 (top), 69 (bottom), 92, 102 (bottom), 173 (bottom), 192 (bottom)
Photographer: Lynne Harrison

Pages 49, 66, 99 (top)
Photographer: R. Todd Davis

Pages 11, 18 (top), 58, 188
Field Editor: Andrea Caughey
Photographer: Ed Gohlich
Landscape Architect: David McCullough, McCullough
Landscape Architecture, 363 5th Ave., Suite 301,
San Diego, CA 92101; 619/296-3150

Pages 107, 109, 132 (top)
Field Editor: Lisa Mowry
Photographer: Emily Followill
Builder: Michael Ladisic, Ladisic Fine Homes, 3133
Maple Dr. NE, Atlanta, GA 30305; 404/495-0708

Pages 13 (right), 150 (left), 179, 187, 192 (top)
Field Editor: Andrea Caughey
Photographer: Ed Gohlich
Deck Builder: Bill White, Bill White Painting and Home
Improvement, 4471 Pocahontas Ave., San Diego, CA
92117; 858/270-4482

GLOSSARY

Actual dimension. The actual size of dimensioned lumber after milling and drying. *See* Nominal Dimension.

Aggregate. The noncement solids used to make concrete. Crushed rock is the coarse aggregate; sand is the fine aggregate.

Anchor. Metal device set in concrete for attaching posts to footings or piers.

Backerboard. A ready-made panel constructed of nylon mesh and a cement or gypsum core; used as a substrate for ceramic tile installations.

Backfill. To replace earth excavated during construction. A material other than the original earth may be used.

Backsplash. The area directly above and behind a countertop. A backsplash can be an integral part of the countertop or fastened to the wall surface.

Baluster. A vertical railing member usually spaced between posts.

Batterboard. A slat fastened horizontally to stakes at a foundation corner. Strings are run between batterboards to mark the perimeter of slabs or foundations.

Beam. A horizontal framing member that usually rests on posts and supports the joists.

Bevel cut. An angle cut through the thickness of a piece of wood.

Blocking. Short pieces of lumber between joists that keep the joists from twisting and strengthen the framing.

Board. A piece of lumber that is less than 2 inches thick and more than 3 inches wide.

Board foot. The standard unit of measurement for wood. One board foot is equal to a piece 12×12×1 inches (nominal size).

Bracing. Diagonal crosspieces nailed and bolted between tall posts, usually those more than 5 feet tall.

Broom finish. A slip-resistant texture made by brushing a stiff broom across fresh concrete.

Building codes. Community ordinances governing the manner in which a home or other structure may be constructed or modified. Most codes deal primarily with fire and health concerns and have separate sections relating to electrical, plumbing, and structural work. *See also* Zoning.

Bull float. A wide, flat tool approximately 3 feet long that is fixed to a pole and used to float concrete slabs before troweling.

Butt. To place materials end-to-end or end-to-edge without overlapping.

Cantilever. A beam or beams projecting beyond a support member.

Casing. Trimming around a door, window, or other opening.

Ceramic tile. Made from refined clay usually mixed with additives and water and hardened in a kiln. Can be glazed or unglazed.

Check. A crack on the surface of a board. A check that runs more than halfway through the thickness of a board weakens the board.

Circuit. The path of electrical flow from a power source through an outlet and back to ground.

Circuit breaker. A switch that automatically interrupts electrical flow in a circuit in case of an overload or short circuit.

Cleat. A short length of lumber attached to strengthen another member or provide a nailing surface.

Codes. *See* Building Codes.

Concrete. A mixture of water, sand, gravel, and portland cement.

Conduit. Rigid or flexible tubing, made of metal or plastic, through which wires and cables are run. Often buried underground when used to convey electrical wire to an outdoor fixture.

Control joint. A narrow groove cut or tooled into a concrete slab to prevent random cracking from shrinkage or stress. Depth is usually about one-fourth of the slab thickness, and joints usually are cut to form square proportions in the slab sections.

Countersink. To drive the head of a nail or screw flush with or slightly below the surface of the wood.

Crook. A bend along the length of a board that is visible by sighting along one edge.

Crosscut. To saw a piece of lumber perpendicular to its length or its grain to reduce its length.

Crown. A slight edgewise bow in a board.

Cup. A curve along the width of a board. Usually not a problem for framing lumber. Slight cupping in decking boards can be corrected by screwing down each side of the board. Reject any boards with severe cupping.

Decking. The boards that make the walking surface of a deck. Decking is usually 2×6, 2×4, or ¾×6 lumber.

Dimension lumber. Lumber at least 2 inches wide and 2 inches thick that has been cut to modular dimensions.

Edging. Wood used as trim to cover the edges of boards, especially decking.

Elevation. A drawn view of the deck or yard that shows a vertical face.

End grain. Wood fibers that are exposed at the ends of boards.

Fascia. Horizontal trim that covers framing right under the decking.

Finial. An ornament attached to the top of a post or peak of an arch.

Flashing. Strips of metal, usually galvanized steel or aluminum, used for weather protection.

Floating. The first step in finishing a concrete surface. It seats the large aggregate below the surface and removes minor irregularities in flatness.

Flush. On the same plane or level with the surrounding surface.

Footing. A small foundation, usually made of concrete, that supports a post.

Frost heave. The movement of ground caused when soil moisture freezes. Posts and footings that do not extend below the frost line are subject to frost heave.

Frost line. The maximum depth at which the ground in an area freezes during winter.

Glazing. A protective and decorative coating, often colored, that is fired onto the surface of some tiles.

Grain. The direction and pattern of fibers in a piece of wood.

Ground fault circuit interrupter (GFCI). An electrical safety device that senses shock hazards and automatically shuts off an electrical circuit. A GFCI can be a circuit breaker in the main panel or a special receptacle used in a kitchen, bathroom, or exterior setting.

Grout. A thin mortar used to fill the joints between tiles; often colored to match or complement the tile.

Hardwood. Lumber that comes from deciduous trees.

Header. A framing member across the ends of the joists.

Heartwood. The center and most durable part of a tree.

Hue. Another word for color, it's most often used to identify a specific shade of a color.

Joist. Horizontal framing members that support decking.

Joist hanger. A metal connector used to join a joist to a ledger or rim joist.

KDAT (Kiln Dried After Treatment). Lumber that has been dried after being treated with preservative; more expensive than pressure-treated lumber but less likely to warp.

Ledger. A horizontal board that supports framing members.

Level. True horizontal. Also a tool used to determine level.

Linear foot. A term used to refer to the length of a board as opposed to board foot.

Load. Weights and forces that a structure is designed to withstand.

Mastic. A thick-body adhesive sometimes used to set ceramic tiles or other surfacing products.

Miter joint. The joint formed when two members meet that have been cut at the same angle (usually 45 degrees).

Molding. Wood that covers exposed edges or serves as decoration.

Nominal dimension. The stated size of a piece of lumber, such as a 2×4 or a 1×12. Actual dimensions are smaller.

On center (OC). The distance from the center of one regularly spaced member to the center of the next.

Outlet. Any potential point of use in a circuit including receptacles, switches, and light fixtures.

Pergola. An open overhead structure designed to provide shade.

Pier. Concrete, usually preformed in a pyramid shape, used to support a post.

Pilot hole. A hole made to prevent splitting the wood when driving a screw or nail.

Plan view. A drawing that shows an overhead view.

Plumb. The condition that exists when a member is at true vertical, pointing to the earth's center of gravity.

Plywood. A building material made of sheets of wood veneer laminated with the grains at 90 degrees to each other.

Post. A vertical framing piece that supports a beam or joist.

Pressure-treated wood. Lumber and sheet goods impregnated with one of several solutions to make the wood more impervious to moisture and weather.

Rail. A horizontal framing member that spans between posts to support balusters and sometimes the rail cap.

Ready-mix concrete. Wet concrete delivered by truck ready to pour.

Rim joist. A joist at the outside edge of a framing layout.

Rip cut. A cut made parallel to the length of a board or its grain to reduce the board's width.

Rise. Total rise is the vertical distance a stairway climbs. Unit rise is the vertical distance between the surfaces of two consecutive treads.

Riser. A board attached to the vertical cut surface of a stair stringer used to cover the gap between treads and provide additional tread support.

Run. Total run is the horizontal distance a stairway spans from the structure to grade. Unit run is the horizontal depth of a tread cut made in a stringer.

Sapwood. The lighter-color recent growth of any species of wood.

Sealer. A protective coating (usually clear) applied to wood or metal.

Set a nail. To drive the head of a nail slightly below the surface of the wood.

Setback. The minimum distance between a property line and any structure as specified by local building and zoning rules.

Site plan. A map of a property that shows major permanent features such as the house, outbuildings, and trees.

Skirt or skirting. Horizontal pieces of lumber installed along the perimeter of a deck to conceal the area below the decking. Skirting may be made of solid boards, either vertical or horizontal, or of lattice, to allow for air movement.

Sleeper. Horizontal wood member laid directly on the ground, a patio, or a roof to support decking.

Softwood. Lumber derived from evergreen trees.

Span. The length of a beam, joist, or decking board between supporting structures.

Square. The condition that exists when one surface is at a 90-degree angle to another. Also a tool used to determine square.

Stringer. A sloping board used to support treads and risers on a stairway. Stringers are usually made of 2×12s.

Substrate. A foundation layer of material upon which another material is installed or fastened.

Thinset mortar. A common setting adhesive for ceramic tiles, it's used to create a bonding layer between the substrate and tile.

Toenail. To drive a nail at an angle to hold together two pieces of material.

Tongue and groove. A joint made using boards that have a projecting tongue on one edge and a matching groove on the opposite edge.

Tuckpointing. The process of refilling old masonry joints with new mortar.

Universal design. The design of products or environments that allows accessibility to all people regardless of age or ability.

Veneer. A thin layer of decorative material such as brick or stone attached to the surface of a base material to serve as a facing.

Vitreous tile. Ceramic tiles with a low porosity, used indoors or outdoors, especially in wet locations such as a patio.

Warp. Any of several lumber defects caused by uneven shrinkage of wood cells during drying.

Zoning. Ordinances regulating the ways in which a property may be used in a given neighborhood. Zoning laws may limit where you can locate a structure.

INDEX

Welcome Home

Stone Landscaping
IDEAS & HOW-TO
Paths · Steps · Patios · Walls

Outdoor Kitchens
IDEAS & HOW-TO
Grills · Fireplaces · Lighting · Landscaping

Garden Structures
IDEAS & HOW-TO
Gazebos · Arbors · Trellises · Pergolas

Expert **advice** + **inspiration** + **ideas** + **how-to** for designing, building, maintaining your home's beautiful exterior